To Doreen
with love and best
wishes,

Alex

Dec 2013

THE
LITTLE
BOOK
OF
LANCASHIRE

ALEXANDER TULLOCH

First published 2013

The History Press
The Mill, Brimscombe Port
Stroud, Gloucestershire, GL5 2QG
www.thehistorypress.co.uk

British Library Cataloguing in Publication Data.
A catalogue record for this book is available from the British Library.

ISBN 978 0 7524 9703 7

Typesetting and origination by The History Press
Printed in Great Britain

CONTENTS

INTRODUCTION

There is more than one Lancashire. There is the 'eee-bah-gum-lass' county of legend, where every man wears a cloth cap, races pigeons, keeps whippets and drinks stout in the pub on a Friday and Saturday night as he enjoys a game of cribbage or shove ha'penny. Then there is the totally different world of the brash, gaudy, 'kiss-me-quick' Lancashire seaside town of Blackpool, with its constant promise of cheap thrills and bawdy entertainment. And both of these stereotypical images stand in sharp contrast to the dark, brooding Pendle Hill which captivates with its strange, eerily fascinating atmosphere and associations with witchcraft and the dark arts.

But we have not finished yet. There is also the Lancashire of outstanding beauty with places such as the Forest of Bowland and the southern tip of the Lake District with scenery to compare with the finest anywhere in the British Isles. Here a traveller can spend hours, days or even longer just gazing into the distance, awestruck by the wonderful views and nature's apparently infinite beneficence in that part of the world. Such breathtaking beauty stands in sharp contrast to yet another Lancashire; the historical Lancashire of the 'dark satanic mills', coal mines and factories where people toiled from dawn till dusk to earn a crust and provide the muscle power to drive the industrial revolution that made Britain the powerful and influential nation it became in the nineteenth and twentieth centuries. Because of the various administrative and commercial decisions that were taken in the 1970s and 1980s much of this industrial Lancashire has either disappeared or is just about hanging on by its finger tips. The majority of the factories, mills and mines have closed, and many of the traditional industries have vanished along with the jobs that provided men and women with the means of making a living. But at least the air is no longer polluted with grime and smoke. Meanwhile, service industries, tourism, and information technology etc. (the newcomers to the market place), offer employers and employees alike greater expectations and a far healthier working environment. Time was when the Lancashire miner would drag himself home after a long shift and scrub the muck off his body in a tin bath in front of the living-room fire. Now people are more likely to drive home from the office, have a meal, check their emails, call a friend or colleague on their mobile phone and then settle down to watch the telly.

And then there is the far more contentious issue of the changes imposed upon the people of the noble and ancient county by politicians who (and I use the expression with considerable hesitation) 'in their wisdom' saw fit to do away with the Lancashire that had survived and prospered since its foundation in the twelfth century. The result is that we now have a situation where traditional Lancashire cities such as Liverpool and Manchester are, officially, no longer part of that fair county. Liverpool has been swallowed up by somewhere called 'Merseyside', and Manchester has been expanded into the amorphous conglomerate of what is now referred to, rather grandiloquently, as the Greater Metropolitan County of Manchester. But most people born within the ancient boundaries of the old county before 1974 still consider themselves Lancastrians. The author of the present volume was born in Liverpool in 1943 and is still proud to consider himself both a Scouser and a Lancastrian; he would never dream of referring to himself as a 'Merseysider'.

The redrawing of the county borders has also had implications for this book. It simply did not seem right, either emotionally or historically, to write a book on the people, places and history of Lancashire without including Manchester, Southport or Liverpool. It would be a nonsense for a book claiming to celebrate the county to omit such worthies as L.S. Lowry (born in Stretford, now part of Greater Manchester), Stan Laurel (born in Ulverston, now within Cumbria) or the steeplejacks' steeplejack Fred Dibnah, who was born in Bolton, a town which, to most people, is still very much part of Lancashire but which has also been absorbed into the great Moloch of Greater Manchester. Needless to say, this historical and political confusion also caused the present author a slight problem; how do you even start to write a book claiming to present the reader with an overview of a county if historically integral parts have to be excluded? The answer was obvious: he simply turned a conveniently blind eye to the changes introduced. Consequently the county

presented in this volume is the *real* Lancashire that existed prior to the unnecessary and, to most people's way of thinking, inexplicable machinations of the politicians in 1974.

On a more personal level, however, the author did find himself confronted with another problem. In the light of his dismissal of the politicians' twentieth-century version of Lancashire, readers might find it a little odd that the mighty port of Liverpool has been somewhat neglected, despite the historically and culturally important role the city played in the development of the country as a whole and the county in particular. The explanation here is quite simple: the city was dealt with fairly comprehensively in an earlier volume by the same author, *The Little Book of Liverpool*. A certain amount of overlap, even repetition, was unavoidable, but it was considered preferable to keep both to an absolute minimum.

1

BEFORE
WE BEGIN

AN ABC OF LANCASHIRE

A is for **Aintree,** now a suburb of Liverpool where the famous horse race, the Grand National is run; Richard **Arkwright,** who invented the 'spinning jenny' and is considered one of those who began the industrial revolution; **Anfield,** the home to Liverpool FC.

B is for **black puddings,** the Lancashire delicacy made from pigs' blood and oats; **Blackpool,** famous for guest houses, Blackpool rock and the illuminations; **Brigantes,** the Celtic tribe which occupied most of what is now Lancashire before the Romans arrived.

C is for *Coronation Street*, the longest running TV soap opera, which was first broadcast on 9 December 1960 and was originally only meant to run for about six weeks; **clog** dancing, a popular pastime in Lancashire, which gave Stan Laurel and **Charlie Chaplin** their entrée into the world of showbiz.

D is for Liverpool **Docks,** which form part of one of the major ports in the whole country; Hilary **Devey,** born in Bolton, successful businesswoman and 'dragon' on the TV show *Dragons' Den*.

E is for **Everton,** a suburb of Liverpool which gave its name to a major football club. The strange thing is, however, that

Everton FC is based in Anfield, as is Liverpool FC. St **Elfin**, obscure saint to whom Warrington Parish Church is dedicated.

F is for Gracie **Fields**, one of the most famous singers and entertainers ever to come out of Lancashire; Andrew 'Freddie' **Flintoff**, born in Preston, played cricket for Lancashire and England.

G is for **Garston**, a part of Liverpool which was the setting for the TV sitcom *Bread*.

H is for **Hale**, a village in the south of the county which is the last resting place of the 9ft 3ins tall giant, John Middleton (1578–1623); the song **Homeward Bound**, which was composed by Paul Simon on Widnes railway station.

I is for **Inglewhite**, a delightful little village, typical of many in the Lancashire Fells, about seven miles outside Preston; John **Inman**, actor, who was born in Preston.

J is for **Jeremiah** Horrocks, who founded a cotton mill in Preston which became one of the biggest in the county and was a major employer in the area at the height of the cotton trade; **Jodrell Bank**, the University of Manchester's observatory, which opened in 1945.

K is for **Knotty Ash**, a real suburb of Liverpool which was made famous by Ken Dodd and his Diddymen. The 'jam butty mines' are, unfortunately, purely fictitious; Wigan-born Roy **Kinnear**, comedy actor.

L is for **Longsight** in Manchester, where Sir Charles Hallé, the founder of the Hallé Orchestra, lived at No. 3 Addison Terrace in 1848; **Lanky**, the term applied by Lancastrians to their own dialect; **Longridge**, where Oliver

Cromwell is reputed to have stayed before the Battle of Preston in 1648.

M is for **Meccano,** the children's construction game, which was devised in 1901 by Frank Hornby, a native of **Maghull;** the **Man and Scythe** in Bolton, which is thought to be the oldest pub in Lancashire – it dates from 1251.

N is for **Newton-le-Willows,** where George Formby (as George Hoy) made his performing debut at the Hippodrome Theatre.

O is for **Old Trafford,** near Manchester, famous for its cricket ground; **Oldham,** the launch pad for Winston Churchill's career in politics; George **Orwell,** who described the plight of people in Lancashire and Yorkshire during the Great Depression in his novel *The Road to Wigan Pier.*

P is for **Preston,** which became Britain's newest city (and the country's fiftieth) in 2002; Robert **Peel,** who hailed from Bury and went on to be the country's youngest prime minister and to establish the first police force.

Q is for Sir Anthony **Quayle**, born in Ainsdale in 1913, the quintessential English actor who seemed to specialise in stiff-upper-lip army-officer roles in the 1950s and '60s; the Lancashire pub with the shortest name in England, '**Q**'.

R is for **Rochdale**, where the modern co-operative movement was started in 1844.

S is for **Scouse**, the Liverpool culinary delicacy and the name by which the local dialect is generally known; **Stretford**, the birthplace of one of Lancashire's most famous sons, L.S. Lowry.

T is for **Tripe and Onions**, another culinary delicacy which, historically, played a major role in feeding the population of Lancashire; **Treales**, a village near Preston with a Welsh name: it is derived from the words *tref*, 'homestead', and *llys*, 'court' or 'manor', and so once was presumably a Celtic settlement belonging to a manor house.

U is for **Ulverston** in the very north of the county and the birthplace of Stan Laurel, one half of the comedy duo Laurel and Hardy; Manchester **United,** one of the most successful football teams in the history of the game.

V is for **Victory-V** lozenges which are manufactured in Lancashire.

W is for **Warrington**, formerly Wilderspool, where King John was informed about a little creek his scouts had found which might make a suitable harbour – that 'little creek' grew into the mighty port of Liverpool; the **Windmill** at Lytham St Annes on the Fylde coast.

X is for 'X' the unknown pleasures and delights that await anybody making his or her first visit to Lancashire.

Y is for the **Yarrow** river and reservoir; Horrocks's **Yellow** Mill in Preston (1792–1942).

Z is for *Z-cars*, the popular 1960s police drama series which was filmed in Lancashire; it is also for the third letter in Fazakerley and the sixth in Anglezarke – Place names in England containing the letter 'z' are very few and far between.

...AND JUST FOR STARTERS

Lancashire is known as 'the Red Rose County'. The Red Rose of Lancaster (sometimes incorrectly referred to as the Red Rose of Lancashire) is the heraldic device of the House of Lancaster. It was adopted as a family emblem by Edmund, First Earl of Lancaster and then became the emblem of Lancashire after the Battle of Bosworth Field in 1485. This was probably a deliberate ploy on

the part of the Earl, who wanted to find some sort of symbol to counterbalance the White Rose of the House of York.

Other names for the rose are: Old Red Damask, the Rose of Provins (an ancient town to the south east of Paris) and the Apothecary's Rose.

The Romans are thought to have brought the rose from Central Asia, where it grew wild, to what we now call France but was then Gaul. This accounts for its scientific name being *Rosa gallica officinalis*.

The adjective *officinalis* tells us that it could be used by herbalists for its medicinal properties, hence its alternative name as the Apothecary's Rose.

Areas of the north-west which are officially no longer part of Lancashire, such as Merseyside and Greater Manchester, still have the Rose of Lancaster incorporated in their coats of arms. The rose also features in the Canadian Army's Saskatoon Light Infantry cap badge.

The flag of Montreal (Canada) also includes the Rose of Lancaster.

Lancaster, Pennsylvania (USA) is known as Red Rose City and has the rose as the design for its seal which reads: LANCASTRA BRITANNIA / LANCASTRA PENNSYLVANIA.

You have to be careful with the word 'maiden' in Lancashire. A tale is often told there about the foreigner (or perhaps just somebody from another part of the country) who was strolling through a Lancashire town and was amazed to see a sign in a shop window which read 'MAIDEN FOR SALE'. He entered the shop keen to inspect the goods only to discover, to his embarrassment (and no doubt disappointment!), that in Lancashire a maiden is not only a sexually inexperienced young lady but also what the rest of the country refers to as a 'clothes horse'.

Lancaster and Lancashire both take their name from the River Lune, which runs from Ravenstonedale in Cumbria through the county to Plover Scar where it flows into Morecambe Bay. The name Lune is almost certainly derived from the Celtic word 'lon' (modern Gaelic 'slan') meaning 'health' or 'safety'. Presumably in the dim and distant past it was thought to be a safe place to bathe or that the water had health-giving properties. Lonsdale, also in Lancashire, takes its name from the same root.

The River Lune is 44 miles long.

WHAT THE ROMANS CALLED THEM

Manchester	Mamucium
Lancaster	Calunium
Ribchester	Bremetanacum Veteranorum
Burrow-in-Lonsdale	Calacum
Castleshaw	Rigodunum
Wigan	Coccium
Morecambe Bay	Moricambe Sinus
Littleborough	Segelocum
Portus Setantorium	Fleetwood (probably)

LANCASHIRE PLACE NAMES AS SURNAMES

There are many towns and cities in Lancashire with names that double up as surnames: Robert **Preston** (actor), Tony **Blackburn** (DJ and TV personality), Valerie **Singleton** (TV personality), Ian **Banks** (footballer), Mike **Leigh** (film director and actor), George **Formby** (film star and banjo player), Bing **Crosby** (American singer and film star), Jimmy **Clitheroe** (1950s radio comedian), Horatio **Nelson** (admiral), Kelly **Holmes** (athlete), Mike **Atherton** (cricketer), Len **Hutton** (cricketer), Myra **Hindley** (mass murderer), Max **Pemberton** (doctor and journalist), Sarah **Lancashire** (actress), Sarah **Lancaster** (American actress), Burt

Lancaster (American actor), Roy **Hattersley** (politician and journalist), Christopher **Eccleston** (actor), Bill **Bowden** (tennis instructor), Victoria **Pendleton** (cyclist), Arthur Hugh **Clough** (educationalist and poet), Robert **Shaw** (actor). Then there is the Liverpool boxer of the 1950s whose Christian name and surname are both Lancashire place names, **Nelson** (aka Nel) **Tarlton**.

It is rumoured that the Queen thinks that the Ribble Valley is the most beautiful part of the country and that she has expressed a wish to retire there.

Dunsop Bridge which is situated in the Ribble Valley is the very centre of the British Isles.

Interested in dinosaurs? Did you know that the man who devised the word was from Lancaster? His name was Richard Owen (1804–1892) and he was one of the world's first palaeontologists. He wanted to find a name for the prehistoric monsters which were being discovered all over the world, and took two Greek words, *deinos* 'terrible' and *sauros* 'lizard', and combined them. So a 'dinosaur' is really a 'terrible lizard'.

The smallest town in England is Bashall, not far from Clitheroe. It is really just a village but it is usually referred to locally as 'Bashall Town'.

When the Pilgrim Fathers set sail to make a new life for themselves in what is now Plymouth, Massachusetts (USA), they hired a professional soldier, a certain Miles Standish, as their guide and military advisor. He was born in Chorley sometime around 1584 and died in Massachusetts, America in 1656.

The delightful old village of Chipping, nestled in the Lancashire Fells a few miles outside of Preston, has several pubs and a quaint little post office, and a shop with a big claim to fame. It is one of the oldest shops in the country and has never ceased trading since it first opened in the 1600s.

In Garstang in October 2007 an event of world-shattering importance took place; the world's biggest Lancashire hotpot was created as a kick-start to the 'Taste Lancashire' celebrations of 2008. The event was considered so important in the social history of the country that it is recorded in the *Guinness Book of Records*.

There is a story, which might or might not be true, that Hoghton Tower near Preston is the birth place of one of England's most traditional meals. It is reputed that James I lodged at the tower sometime in 1617 and was so impressed by the loin of beef he was given for dinner that he took out his sword there and then and knighted it. This is supposed to be the origin of the culinary term 'a sirloin' of beef.

Pendle Hill, just outside Preston, is just 175ft too short to be called a mountain. It is 1,835ft above sea level and a mountain is only a mountain if it is 2,000ft above sea level or more.

According to legend, King Arthur's mighty sword Excalibur is lying at the bottom of Lancashire's deepest lake, Martin Mere. Another legend claims that King Arthur fought his tenth battle on the nearby banks of the River Ribble, so there might just be a connection.

The founder of the Quaker movement, George Fox, is reputed to have had a traumatic religious experience (some say a vision) on Pendle Hill in 1652.

Garstang, near Preston, was the world's very first Fair Trade town.

Question: Why do we talk about the Lancashire 'fells' when we mean hills?
Answer: Because the word 'fell' is derived from the Old Norse *fjall*, meaning 'hill'. It is a hangover from the days when Lancashire was settled by the Norse-speaking Vikings.

The tallest spire of any parish church in England is that of St Walburge's in Preston. St Walburge (or, more correctly, St Walburga) was born somewhere in Devon about the year AD 710.

St Walburge is the patron saint of people suffering from rabies.

The architect responsible for St Walburge's church was the York born architect J.A. Hansom, the same man who designed the Hansom cab in 1834.

The iconic British film *Brief Encounter*, starring Trevor Howard and Celia Johnson, was filmed on Carnforth station early in 1945. The reason for the choice of location had nothing to do with the storyline or the beauty of the surrounding countryside. It was chosen simply because it was feared that the bright lights used in filming might have attracted German bombers if the film had been set nearer to London. With hindsight, the measures taken smack of over-caution as the Luftwaffe was a bit of a spent force by then.

Emmeline Pankhurst (née Goulden) was born in Moss Side, Manchester, in 1858. She was the leader of the Suffragettes who fought for, and eventually won, the right for women in Britain to vote.

The Mersey Ferry

There can be few people alive who have not heard the Gerry and the Pacemakers' song 'Ferry Cross the Mersey'. The ferry in question, of course, is the ferry boat which has conveyed travellers from the southern tip of Lancashire over to the Wirral for centuries.

The service was begun in the twelfth century when the Benedictine monks from the priory in Birkenhead spotted a gap in the market. They no doubt decided that they could demonstrate their Christian concern for their fellow men but at the same time earn a few coppers for themselves. So they began rowing wayfarers to and from the Pool (modern Whitechapel / Paradise Street in Liverpool) for a modest fee, and the service has continued ever since. Nowadays, however, passengers enjoy the comparative comfort of a modern boat and the crew is no longer comprised of Benedictine monks!

LANCASHIRE'S HERALDIC MOTTOES

Lancashire County Council – *In Concilio Consilium* (in council is wisdom)

Blackburn and Darwen – *Arte et Labore* (by skill and labour)

Bolton Metropolitan Council – Progress

Burnley Borough Council – *Supera moras* (overcome delays)

Bury Metropolitan Borough Council – Forward in Unity

Chorley Borough Council – Be Aware

Fylde Borough Council – *Gaudeat ager* (let the field [or fylde] be joyful)

Hyndburn Borough Council – By Industry and Prudence

Knowsley Metropolitan Borough Council – By Faith and Industry

Lancaster City Council – Luck to Loyne (ie the River Lune)

Liverpool City Council – *Deus Nobis Haec Otia Fecit* (God has granted us this ease)

Manchester City Council – *Concilio et Labore* (by council and labour)

Oldham Metropolitan Borough Council – *Sapere Aude* (dare to know)

Pendle Borough Council – *In unitate florescemus* (in unity we flourish)

Rossendale Borough Council – Prosperity through Endeavour

St Helens Metropolitan Borough Council – *Prosperitas in Excelsis* (flourishing well)

Salford City Council – *Salus Populi Suprema Lex* (the welfare of the people is the highest law)

South Ribble Borough Council – Progress with Humanity

Stockport Borough Council – With Courage and Faith

Tameside Metropolitan Borough Council – Industry and Integrity

Trafford Metropolitan Borough Council – Hold Fast That Which Is Good

West Lancashire District Council – *Salus Populi Suprema Lex* (the welfare of the people is the highest law)

Wyre Borough Council – *Ultraque parte fluminis* (and on the other side of the river)

Clitheroe Town Council – *Stabit Saxum Fluit Amnis* (the rock will remain and the river will flow)
Morecambe Town Council – Beauty Surrounds, Health Abounds

Preston is bit of an anomaly when it comes to heraldic mottoes. The Preston Borough Council's coat of arms bears no motto, but it does display the initials PP. They are frequently taken to stand for Proud Preston, but this is a mistake – the initials stand for *Princeps Pacis* (Prince of Peace), a title bestowed on St Wilfrid (*c.* AD 633–709) the patron saint of Preston.

St Wilfrid is also the patron saint of reformers.

The poet Robert Service (1874–1958), otherwise known as the Bard of the Yukon, was born in Preston and lived for a while in Winckley Street. His most famous poems are 'The Shooting of Dan McGrew' and 'The Cremation of Sam McGee'.

Britain's first electric tram, which revolutionised transport in the whole country, made its début appearance on the streets of Blackpool on 29 September 1885.

Are you a fan of the *Star Wars* films? Did you know that inside the android R2-D2 is the dwarf actor Kenny Baker. He was born in Preston in 1934.

Clogs, as just about every man and his dog knows, were once the preferred footwear for many people in Lancashire, particularly with those who worked in the mills. They were made of wood and leather with plenty of steel nails holding everything together. But for many people they also served as a kind of timepiece. The inhabitants of the mill towns could hear the mill workers clattering along the cobbles to and from the mills at set times of the day, and so did not need a watch (which few could afford to buy) to know what time of day it was. In fact, you could 'set your clock by them' if you had one.

But the origin of the humble clog is not to be found at the cobbler's workbench but on the farm. In the fourteenth century if a farmer wanted his horse to slow down for any reason he would tie a heavy lump of wood, known in Middle English as a *clogge,* to one or more of its hooves. Later on somebody had the idea of making shoes out these *clogges* and so the idea of the modern clog was born. The fact that these lumps of wood acted as a sort of hindrance or impediment to movement is why we can now talk of something being 'clogged' up.

In the heyday of the Blackpool landlady, particularly in the 1930s and '40s, it was widely accepted that she ruled the roost. Guests might have been on holiday (or even on a honeymoon!) but they still had to live by what might now seem like very rigid rules: meal times were strictly adhered to, the front door was often locked at ten o'clock at night and guests were expected to leave after breakfast and were not allowed back until the evening. If guests wanted to have a bath they had to give twenty-four hours' notice and unbelievably, if they wanted to season their evening meal with salt and pepper there would be an extra weekly charge (usually about 12p in today's money) 'for the use of the cruet'.

But the most surprising thing about staying in a boarding house was that food was not usually provided. Guests were expected to bring their own food; all the landlady did was cook it. Imagine that today!

Lancashire, like most parts of the country, has produced many folk remedies for the various aches and pains that afflicted the population in the days when penicillin did not exist and going to the doctor was too expensive. In some parts of the county, for instance, a cure for tonsillitis (supposedly!) was to take a potato, boil it, then cut it in two. Both halves were then wrapped in a flannel and tied to the patient's neck.

And here's another good bit of Lancashire folk medicine. Before the days of central heating it could be pretty cold and damp in a lot of houses, and phlegm, sore throats and bad coughs were frequent problems during the winter. One way of dealing with them was to place a cup in a basin of hot water and put a spoonful of black treacle, a knob of butter and a spoonful of vinegar in it. These were then mixed together until they formed a thick paste which was eaten while still warm. It usually proved to be very efficacious.

Blackpool has a direct linguistic counterpart over the water in Ireland. The capital of the Republic of Ireland is Dublin, the etymology of which is the Irish Gaelic *dubh* 'black' and *linn* 'pool'. Put them together and you get *Dubhlinn* (anglicised as Dublin) which literally means 'Blackpool'.

Chetham's library in Manchester is the oldest surviving public library in England. It was founded in 1653 (although the building in which it is housed dates back to 1421) and visitors today can still see the very table at which Karl Marx (1818–1883) and Friedrich Engels (1820–1895) sat and read when they were gathering information for their major work *The Communist Manifesto*.

The Lancashire cotton mills were a very dangerous place to work, and the only 'health and safety' rules were based on the mill workers' own common sense. One ever-present danger for women was the possibility of getting long hair tangled in the machinery, as this could (and frequently did) result in the hair and scalp being torn right off. To prevent this, the women would wear their hair tightly swept back, tied up and kept well away from the endlessly revolving wheels and unforgiving spinning looms. But at the end of a shift and on their days off the women could 'let their hair down' and relax, hence the expression which has found its way into common parlance.

SOME EYE-CATCHING PUB NAMES IN LANCASHIRE

The Duck and Puddle (Blackburn)
Hark to Bounty (Slaidburn)
Fibber McGees (Lancaster)
Tinker and Bidget (Oswaldtwistle)
Doctor Syntax (Preston)
Hand and Dagger (Kirkham)
Snig's Foot (Ormskirk)
The Cock and Bottle (Tarleton)
The Crooked Billet Inn (Worsthorne)
Clog and Billycock (Blackburn)
The Swan with Two Necks (Pendleton)
The Help me Through (Bury)
The Pig on the Wall (Droylsden)
The Shoulder of Mutton (Holcombe village)
The Pipe and Gannex (Knowsley)
Who'd a Thowt It (Middleton)
Sally Up Steps (Bolton)
The Lion of Vienna (Bolton)
The Strawberry Duck (Entwistle)
The Oxnoble (Manchester)
The Jabez Clegg (Manchester University campus)

The pub with the longest name in England is in Stalybridge: The Old Thirteenth Cheshire Astley Volunteer Rifleman Corps.

And so is the pub with the shortest name: Q.

And the St George Hotel in Kirkham is usually referred to as: The Sticky Clog.

The popular pub name The Eagle and Child, which can be seen throughout Lancashire, is said to originate from a rather unusual tale. This is how it goes:

One of the most influential families in ancient Lancashire was the Lathom family and one of their number, Sir Thomas Lathom, according to tradition, is responsible for a legend concerning the miraculous birth of a child in Lathom Park near Skelmersdale.

The story goes that Sir Thomas was desperate for a son and heir but his wife only produced a series of daughters. In order

to increase his chances of having a son the poor man was driven to indulging in a bit of a dalliance with a local peasant girl who dutifully gave birth to a fine, healthy boy. However Sir Thomas now had to find a way of persuading his wife to accept the child at the same time as not letting her know about his extra-curricular activities. The plan he dreamed up was ingenious. He arranged for the child to be placed in a basket under a tree in the gardens surrounding the manor house, close to where he knew his wife liked to take her daily walk. Then surprise, surprise ... she heard a baby crying just as she walked past. Lady Lathom was delighted and Thomas was able to convince her that an eagle must have brought the child down from Heaven for them and that this was indeed the male heir they had both longed for. She believed her husband's version of events and, as far as we know, they all lived happily ever after.

The 'eagle and child' is still part of the Lathom family crest.

Until very recently there was a pub in Bolton with a very long history and a gruesome claim to fame. Ye Olde Man and Scythe (originally named The Man and Scythe Inn) was founded in 1251, and so qualifies as one of the oldest pubs in the country. During the Civil War, Thomas Stanley, Earl of Derby was kept there by his Parliamentarian captors and then, on the morning of 15 October 1651, he was taken out and beheaded right in front of the pub.

In 1794, in Walton-le-Dale, just outside Preston, an event took place which was the have a serious knock-on effect through the generations and has left a bad taste in the mouths of those who enjoy the odd tipple. That event was the birth of one Joseph Livesey. He grew up to be a successful local businessman who made a killing selling cheese, and at the same time espoused the doctrines of vegetarianism. He was also against the selling and imbibing of strong liquor, so he founded the Preston Temperance Society and took it upon himself to persuade as many people as possible to sign 'The Pledge' and swear that they would 'abstain totally' from booze.

His followers thus became known as 'totallers', but at one of their meetings a certain Dick Turner, who suffered from a bad stammer, swore that he would be 'reet down out-and-out t-totaller for ever and ever', and the term stuck. Joseph Livesey died in 1884.

NOT SO VERY LONG AGO

Very few people had bathrooms and if you wanted a bath you brought the tin bath in from the yard and had your bath in front of the living-room fire.

Those people who had a proper bath often used it for storing the coal.

Few families could afford meat for everyone. If the father was in work he would be given meat with his evening meal with the rest of the family living on bread and potatoes. The reasoning behind the custom was that the father needed to preserve his strength to keep working.

For many families the staple part of the diet was just bread and beef dripping, sprinkled with salt.

For a sweeter snack, many kids in Lancashire used to be given 'sugar butties'. As the name implies these consisted of nothing more than a couple of slices of bread with a sprinkling of sugar for the filling.

Hiring Fairs were a common and popular meeting place both for people looking for work and for potential employers. The practice continued until the First World War.

As late as the 1950s, school classrooms in many Lancashire schools were still lit by gaslight. Moreover, many of them were heated by open coal fires.

Up until the 1950s, most schoolchildren were still learning to write using chalk and a slate board. In the more technologically advanced schools children learned to write with a steel-nib pen which had to be dipped into an ink-well fitted in the desk.

The highlight of everybody's year were the Wakes Weeks, when the mills would shut down and the workers would set off for a week at the seaside, usually visiting places such as Blackpool, Southport or Morecambe.

The expression 'to mug somebody' meant to treat them to a cup of tea. It had nothing to do with beating them up and stealing their money.

In the Lancashire mill towns there was one tradesman who was almost always guaranteed employment: the knocker-up. It was his job to walk the streets very early in the morning with a long pole, which he used for tapping on bedroom windows. When an alarm clock was beyond the means of most workers, this was the only way they could make sure they did not oversleep. Oversleeping meant being late for work and that could mean being sacked.

Most houses had a 'petty', the Lanky term for a toilet. But it was nearly always outside the house and across the backyard; the inside toilet, like the bathroom, was a much later development. This frequently meant that performing natural functions in winter was done under freezing conditions and in summer the smell was disgusting, not to mention the bluebottles!

Just about everyone shopped at 'the Co-op'. Every member had his or her own personal number (the forerunner of the PIN) which had to be given every time a purchase was made in a Co-op shop. The amount spent was then recorded by the shop-keeper and every three months a dividend (usually known as the 'divi') was paid back to the customer.

Fish and chip shops were just that – they sold fish (cod or haddock) and chips and nothing else.

Before the American craze of 'trick or treat' came to these shores, Halloween was also known in parts of Lancashire as 'Duck Apple Night'. People would gather around a tin bath containing about six inches of water with apples floating on the top and everyone had to 'duck' for an apple, i.e. try to get one out of the bath using only the mouth, with your hands tied behind your back.

In the days before everybody had a fridge, some weird and wonderful ways had to be found for keeping food fresh. To stop milk curdling it was the custom in Lancashire to stand the bottles of milk in a bowl of water and cover them with a damp cloth. It did work, but not for very long.

Kids would play hopscotch and skipping games in the street. Boys used to play cricket using the lamp posts as the wickets.

In the days before people had washing machines, wives and mothers had to wash the family clothes in a 'dolly tub' using a lot of elbow grease and a 'posser' (a hand-held device for churning the clothes inside the tub). Alternatively, they could make use of a local laundry. This usually involved wrapping the dirty clothes in a sheet, attaching a list of all the clothes and then carrying the bundle to the local laundry and collecting it, nicely laundered, a few days later.

In the days when coal mining was a thriving industry in Lancashire the miners hardly ever saw daylight. They would make their way down to the coalface before dawn and would not emerge again until after sunset. So, obviously, they had to take enough food with them to last for the whole of the shift, and this pack of 'butties' (sandwiches), carried in a little tin strapped to their belts, was called 'snap' or 'baggin'. If a miner got to the pithead and realised he had forgotten his snap, it was considered bad luck to go back for it so he had to go without any food all day.

In Liverpool the dockers also took their butties to work in a little tin, but their term for it was a 'growler'.

The Rose and Crown pub in Hoole, near Preston, has some gruesome associations. It was bought and taken over in 1952 by Albert Pierrepoint, Britain's last hangman. Some of the regulars used to claim that he had a sign on the wall saying 'No hanging around the bar,' but he always denied this.

What has to be one of the strangest names for a road anywhere can be seen in the little village of Banks just outside Southport. 'Ralph's Wife's Lane' takes its name from the story of a fisherman called Ralph who was drowned some time in the eighteenth century when out fishing on the nearby river. His widow was said to have run up and down the lane calling out for her husband until she went mad and died of a broken heart.

George Bradshaw, whose railway timetable guide was made famous by Michael Portillo in his enormously popular and successful television series, Great British Railway Journeys, was born in Pendleton in 1801.

In Lancashire a clough (a word which appears in many place names) is a steep sided valley or ravine

WHY IS THE ROYAL AIR FORCE UNIFORM BLUE?

Some people think that the RAF uniform is blue because of some romantic connection between flying and the deep blue yonder. But the real answer is far more terrestrial. At about the time that the RAF was formed in 1918, a Lancashire firm had recently obtained an order to produce vast amounts of light blue material for uniforms for the Tsar's Imperial cavalry. But when the revolution in Russia occurred the order fell through and the firm was left with thousands of pounds worth of material on its hands. In order to minimise its losses the firm came to an arrangement with the officers of the new force (they had to buy their own uniforms) and so the material and colour became *de rigueur* for the RAF.

THEY WERE BORN IN LANCASHIRE AND YOU'VE SEEN THEM ON TV

Zoe Ball, presenter, Blackpool, b. 1970
Jim Bowen, comedian, Accrington, b. 1939
Steve Coogan, comedian, Middleton, b. 1965
Les Dawson, comedian, Manchester, b. 1931
Chris Evans, chat-show host, Warrington, b. 1966
Anna Friel, actress, Rochdale, b. 1976
Mike Harding, writer and entertainer, Manchester, b. 1944
John Inman, actor, Preston, 1935–2007
Sue Johnston, actress, Warrington, b. 1943
Peter Kay, comedian, Bolton, b. 1973
Vernon Kay, presenter, Bolton, b. 1974
Bert Kwouk, actor, Manchester, b. 1930
Bernard Manning, comedian, Ancoats, 1930–2007
Mystic Meg, fortune teller, Accrington, b. 1942
Bill Oddie, writer, actor, bird-watcher, Rochdale, b. 1941
Arlene Phillips, dancer, Prestwich, b. 1943
Lisa Riley, actress, Bury, b. 1976
Anne Robinson, journalist, TV presenter, Crosby, b. 1944
Nick Robinson, political commentator, Macclesfield, b. 1963
Philip Schofield, presenter, Manchester, b. 1962
John Thaw, actor, Manchester, 1942–2002
Victoria Wood, actress, comedienne, Prestwich, b. 1953

DO YOU UNDERSTAND LANKY?

If you live in Lancashire you probably know these expressions, but if you are a visitor it might come in handy to learn a few. Otherwise communication with the natives could be a little difficult.

Are thee reet? – Do you feel alright?

Well, I'll go to the foot of our stairs! – My word! That does surprise me!

Well, I'll go to our 'ouse! My word! – That does surprise me!

By 'eck! – Good heavens!

Willieckerslike! – He certainly will not!

Er's got a face like a bag o' broken glass – That lady is not very attractive

Wossupwithee? – What is the matter with you?

Cloditint bin – Will you put this in the bin, please?

Thee 'ouse needs a good bottomin' – The house is in need of a thorough cleaning

The Brush

There is an interesting derivation of the Lancastrian expression 'daft as a brush'. The brush in question is not the type used for sweeping and cleaning; it is a reference to a fox's tail. Foxes' 'brushes' are known to be very soft so to say that something is as 'soft as a brush' is to merely point out that the material or object in question is pleasantly yielding to the touch. But 'soft' can also be used to mean 'soft in the head' or 'not very intelligent' and a synonym for 'soft' in this context, in Lancashire, is 'daft'.

A brush also figures in another old Lancashire saying. If a man and woman were living together in a state of unmarried bliss, it used to be said of them that they were 'living o'er t'brush'. This was a reference to their unconventional choice of wedding ceremony. Instead of a church service the couple would simply gather a few friends around for a bit of a party and then the ceremony would take place. The ceremony itself was not complicated in the least, a friend would hold a brush handle a few inches off the floor and the couple, holding hands, would jump over it. Then hey-presto, they considered themselves married.

Another quaint Lancashire custom involving the brush was this: if a woman's husband was working nights she might hang a brush in the front room window. This was understood to mean to passers-by that there was 'half a bed for hire'.

Tha knows – As I am sure you are aware
Tha'll not get owt for nowt – Nothing is free in this world
Eee, that lad's keck 'anded – That young man is left handed/not very good with his hands
'Ee's gone t'petty –He has gone to the toilet
This taste's waller – There is very little flavour in this meal
'Ee's popped 'is clogs – He has died
Ee lad, put wood int' ole – Young man, would you be so good as to close the door?
Ah'l do it mi sen – I'll do it myself
Ah bought this ont' strap – I bought this on credit
Tha's a bit nowty t'day – You're not in a very good mood today
They don't have pockets in shrouds tha' knows! – Spend it before you die!
'Er's nobbut a slip of a lass – She's just a young girl
Anyroad, as ah wuz sayin' – Anyway, as I was saying
Ee, lad, that's gradely – That is wonderful, my friend
Tha's as daft as a brush – You are not very intelligent
It's in fine fettle – It's in good condition
Ah'll soon fettle it – I will soon sort it out/mend it
It's a bit parky out – It's rather cold outside
Ginnel – Alleyway, passageway
That lad's a rum-un – The boy is very lively
Ee fair stinks o' brass – He's rich
Ah'm fair clemmed – I am very hungry

WHOSE TOWN TWINS YOURS?

Preston – Almelo (Netherlands); Kalisz (Poland); Nimes (France); Recklinghausen (Germany)
Blackburn – Péronne (France); Altena (Germany); Tarnow (Poland)
Blackpool – Bottrop (Germany)
Bolton – Le Mans (France); Paderborn (Germany)
Burnley – Vitry-sur-Seine (France)
Bury – Angoulême, Tulle (France); Schorndorff (Germany); Woodbury (USA); Datong (China)

Carnforth – Sailly-sur-la-Lys (France)
Caton with Littledale – Socx (France)
Clitheroe – Rivesaltes (France)
Chorley – Szekesfehérvár (Hungary)
Fleetwood – Fleetwood (USA)
Lancaster – Aalborg (Denmark); Rendsburg (Germany); Växjö (Sweden); Lublin (Poland); Perpignan(France)
Liverpool – Cologne (Germany); Dublin (Republic of Ireland); Shanghai (China); Rio de Janeiro (Brazil)
Manchester – Bilwi (Nicaragua); Chemnitz (Germany); Kanpur (India); Córdoba (Spain); Rehovot (Israel); St Petersburg (Russia); Wuhan (China); Faisalabad (Pakistan); Los Angeles (USA)
Oswaldtwistle – Falkenberg (Sweden)
Rochdale – Bielefeld (Germany); Tourcoing (France); Sahiwal (Pakistan)
Rossendale – Bocholt (Germany)
Salford – Clermont-Ferrand (France)
St Helens – Calon-sur-Saône (France); Stuttgart(Germany)
West Lancashire – Cergy-Pontoise (France); Erkrath (Germany)

THEY ARE NOT ALONE...

Many towns and cities in Lancashire have their counterparts in other parts of the world. Interestingly, most of the namesakes are in America. This is almost certainly an indication of the origin of the early settlers in the New World.

There is a Lancaster in:

New Hampshire, USA
Massachusetts, USA
New York State, USA
Ohio, USA
Pennsylvania, USA
Kentucky, USA
Wisconsin, USA

And a Bolton in:
  East Lothian, Scotland
  Ontario, Canada
  Vermont, USA
  Massachusetts, USA
  Connecticut, USA
  North Carolina, USA
  Mississippi, USA

And a Manchester in:
  New Hampshire, USA
  Connecticut, USA
  New York State, USA
  Iowa, USA
  Georgia, USA

And a Southport in:
  Newfoundland, Canada
  New York State, USA
  North Carolina, USA
  Indiana, USA
  Florida, USA
  Queensland, Australia

And a Salford in:
  Oxfordshire
  Buckinghamshire
  Pennsylvania (USA)
  Ontario (Canada)
  (There is also a Salford near Milton Keynes)

Modern transport in Lancaster, Pennsylvania, USA for the Amish community.

But the one that takes the prize for the most ubiquitous place name has to be **Preston**. In addition to the one in Lancashire there is also:

Preston in: Gloucestershire, two in Devon, one in each
  of Dorset, Yorkshire, Hertfordshire, Northumberland,
  Rutland, Somerset, Tyne-and-Wear, and then three in
  Wiltshire.
In Australia there is a **Preston** in: Victoria, Tasmania,
  Queensland.
In Canada there is a **Preston** in: Nova Scotia (as well as an
  East Preston and a **North Preston**) and in Ontario.
In Scotland there is a **Preston** in: the Scottish Borders and in
  East Lothian.
In America there is a **Preston** in: Connecticut, Georgia,
  Idaho, Indiana, Kansas, Kentucky, Maryland, Minnesota,
  Mississippi, Missouri, Nebraska, Nevada, New York,
  North Carolina, Oklahoma, Texas, Washington, and two
  in Wisconsin.

(This list is by no means exhaustive and does not include the use of the name Preston in compound place names such as **Preston Gubbals** (Shropshire), **Preston-on-the-Hill** (Cheshire) and many more.)

WHO KNEW?

In the coastal town of Heysham there are some ruins which are known as St Patrick's Chapel. Tradition has it that they are all that remains of a small church erected by followers of the saint to mark the spot where he came ashore after being shipwrecked in Morecambe Bay. Modern research also suggests that St Patrick, who went on to become the patron saint of Ireland, was born a few miles further north in what is now Ravenglass [known to the Romans as Glanoventa] in the Lake District.

27 November

Since 1996 the people of the county have been celebrating their birthright on 27 November, by holding 'Lancashire Day'. The date was chosen as it is the anniversary of the day in 1295 when, at the behest of King Edward I, selected men of Lancashire travelled down to London where they were to represent their county at what has come to be known as the Model Parliament.

As part of the celebrations, Lancastrians are expected to indulge in some traditional Lancashire fare and listen to the town criers as they read out the proclamation explaining the significance of the day. Then, at precisely nine o'clock in the evening, all Lancastrians, wherever they might be, are invited to raise a glass and join in a toast to 'The Queen, Duke of Lancaster'.

The savoury dish, consisting of sausages cooked in batter is fairly popular throughout the whole of England, but it was originally a Lancashire dish known as 'frog int 'ole'.

In the 1960s, the pop scene, as everyone knows, was dominated by The Beatles and a myriad of other Liverpool groups. The first group outside 'the Pool' to enjoy any kind of universal acclaim and success were Freddie and the Dreamers who hailed from Manchester.

Most people would expect a forest to have lots of trees, but in places such as the Forest of Bowland there is hardly a tree in sight and much of the area is a vast tract of almost barren gritstone hills and peat moorland. The reason for this is both linguistic and historical. The word 'forest' derives from the Latin *foris* which simply means 'outside' or 'out of doors', so the original idea of a 'forest' was land outside the towns and villages. After the Norman Conquest the term was used to designate areas of countryside which the king or local baron had set aside for hunting. Such hunting 'forests' were established around Trawden, Pendle, Bleasdale, Fullwood, Toxteth and Wyresdale.

In Roman times, the Ribble river, which flows through a large tract of Lancashire and on which Preston stands, was known as the *Belisama*. The name is thought to come from the Celtic goddess of the same name, who was frequently associated with rivers, lakes, fire and light. In Brythonic, the language of the ancient Britons, the word *belisama* is thought to have meant 'summer brightness'.

Stonyhurst College, which lies in the shadow of Pendle Hill, is thought by many to have been the inspiration for Tolkien's *The Lord of the Rings*. This is quite possibly true, as Tolkien's son was a pupil at the college and he is known to have visited him there on many occasions.

2

LANCASHIRE'S TIMELINE

10,000 BC: Evidence of human activity in the area of Poulton-le-Fylde near Preston.

3000 BC: Evidence of primitive settlements at Calderstones, near Liverpool.

AD 43–fifth century: Roman settlements in Lancashire. One such early settlement is thought to have been a large stockade near where modern Lancaster stands.

Around AD 900: Vikings arrive and settle in places around the Mersey and further inland in Lancashire.

1066: Lancaster, established during the Roman occupation of Britain, was given to Roger de Poitou by William the Conqueror as a gift, for services rendered during the conquest.

1179: King Henry II grants Preston its Charter.

1182: Lancashire is established.

1193: Lancaster receives its first charter allowing it to hold markets and fairs.

1207: King John lays the foundations of modern Liverpool and grants the future city its first charter.

1230: Salford granted its charter.

1246: Wigan granted its charter.

1267: Edmund, the son of Henry III, becomes the first Earl of Lancaster.

1282: Manchester mentioned as having a market.

1301: Manchester granted its charter.

1351: Henry, Edmund's grandson, becomes the first Duke of Lancaster.

1362: John of Gaunt becomes the second Duke of Lancaster.

1399: King Richard II seizes the duchy of Lancaster on the death of John of Gaunt.

1421: Church established in Manchester which developed into what is now Manchester Cathedral.

1455: First battle in the War of the Roses between the houses of York and Lancaster.

1485: Battle of Bosworth marks the end of the War of the Roses.

1605: Serious outbreak of plague in Manchester.

1612: Lancaster Castle sees the trial of the Pendle Witches.

1644/45: Serious outbreak of the plague in Liverpool.

1645: Manchester hit by the plague again.

1647: Ormskirk ravaged by the plague.

1648: Royalist Scottish army defeated by Oliver Cromwell at Preston.

1650: Plague breaks out in Warrington and Preston.

1664: George Fox imprisoned in Lancaster for refusing to accept the Oath of Supremacy.

1715: The Jacobite army arrives in Lancaster before setting off for the Battle of Preston.

1745: Bonny Prince Charlie occupies Lancaster.

1761: The Bridgewater Canal opens.

1776: The Bridgewater Canal extended and now links Manchester with Liverpool.

1780: Richard Arkwright commences work on the construction of Manchester's first cotton mill.

1796: The medieval Great Hall in Lancaster Castle is demolished.

1826: Riots on the streets of Lancaster against power looms.

1839: First Grand National run at Aintree.

1844: The Co-operative movement opens its first store in Rochdale.

1846: Carnforth Station opened by the Lancaster and Carlisle Railway.

1853: Manchester is granted city status.

1880: Liverpool is granted city status.

1894: The Manchester Ship Canal opens and Blackpool Tower is completed.

1899: John Rylands Library is founded in Manchester.

1916–18: German POWs incarcerated in Lancaster Castle.

1937: Lancaster is granted city status.

1956: Premium Bonds go on sale administered from St Anne's-on-Sea.

1960: First episode of *Coronation Street*, set in Salford, is broadcast.

1965: Opening of the Pennine Way.

1966: Lancaster University opens its doors to students.

1996: IRA bomb causes havoc and destruction in central Manchester.

1997: IRA bomb hoax causes cancelation of the Grand National.

2002: Preston is granted city status.

2008: Liverpool becomes the 'Capital of Culture'.

2013: Manchester United wins Premier League championship for a record-breaking twentieth time.

LANCASHIRE ... A POTTED HISTORY

AD 34–fifth century: When the Romans arrived they found this part of Britannia a sparsely populated, bleak area, dominated by the Celtic tribe known as the Brigantes. They were a somewhat warlike lot who had done much to impede the Roman progress north. Eventually they were subdued and the Romans started erecting forts wherever suitable or practical. Some of these forts developed into the important industrial and commercial towns and cities dotted about modern Lancashire.

Post fifth century: The Romans left in a bit of a hurry when the legions were needed to defend Rome against the barbarian hordes threatening to destroy the Empire. For a while the land we now call Lancashire was dominated by a Celtic-speaking Romano-British tribe known as the Cumbri. These are the people who gave Cumbria its name.

Around 700: The Anglo-Saxons now began to appear north of the River Mersey. They had already begun to convert to Christianity and brought their beliefs to the Celtic north. By 680, St Cuthbert had established a ministry in Cartmel. Place names ending in -eccles or -ecles (meaning church) indicate Saxon settlements.

Around 900: The Vikings (or Norsemen) arrived along the north-west coast and moved inland. They settled and mixed with the local population, bringing distinctly Scandinavian sounding place names to the area, such as *Birkidalr (*Birkdale); *Krossnes* (Crossens); *Lágrland* (Leyland); *Skarbrekka* (Scarisbrick); *Altkjarr* (Altcar) and *Einulfsdalr* (Ainsdale).

1066: William I (the Conqueror) arrived in England and ushered in huge social changes. The laws of the land were changed, castles sprang up everywhere and Norman French became the language of the court and ruling echelons of society. Although the term Lancashire did not yet exist, the area did begin to develop, not least because of the many abbeys and priories founded in places such as Lancaster, Cockersand, Furness, Cartmel, Whalley Penwortham and Burscough.

1086: Domesday Book was compiled. William's commissioners reported back to him that much of the land between the Mersey and the Ribble was inhospitable wasteland. Nevertheless, places such as West Derby, Toxteth, Smithdown and Speke were included in the book. Preston was mentioned, as was Lancaster, spelled 'Lonecaestre' and Manchester appeared as 'Mamecestre'.

1182: The area '*inter ripam et mersham*' (between the Ribble and the Mersey') became a county in its own right known as Lancashire.

1207: King John I founded the borough of Liverpool as a port of embarkation for his troops en route for Ireland.

1235: The Sherriff of Lancaster, William de Ferrers, completed the construction of Liverpool Castle. It soon became the residence of the Molyneux family, one of Lancashire's most powerful dynasties.

1455–85: The Wars of the Roses in which the houses of Lancaster and York engaged in a power struggle for the crown. Although the period of conflict covered thirty years it was not a time of continuous warfare; it was more a series of often very brutal clashes interspersed with long periods of relative peace. The end came when Henry Tudor defeated the forces of Richard III at Bosworth in 1484 and ushered in the Tudor dynasty. Henry was of the Lancastrian persuasion and so, symbolically, the 'red rose' triumphed over the 'white rose'.

1581: In the sixteenth century, when religious intolerance was the rule and Catholics and Protestants took turns to burn each other at the stake, the Jesuit Edmund Campion fell foul of Queen Elizabeth's dislike of Rome and was hanged, drawn and quartered at Tyburn on 1 December. Bizarrely, and somewhat gruesomely, the ropes used in his execution are preserved to this day in a glass display case in Stonyhurst College in the Lancashire Fells.

1612: The trial of the Pendle Witches at Lancaster Castle. In an age of superstition, when just about any misfortune could be, and frequently was, attributed to anyone and everyone who did not adhere to 'normal' standards of social behaviour, the old beggar women of Pendle stood no chance. Of the ten accused, nine were hanged and the tenth died whilst being held in a cell prior to the trial.

1642–60: The English Civil War affected Lancashire quite badly. As the country divided itself into the supporters of the Royalists and Parliamentarians, Lancashire found itself also torn apart. Roughly speaking, the northern half of the county (Lancaster, Preston etc.) supported the King and the southern half supported Parliament. In the natural ebb and flow of war, some towns and cities changed sides on more than one occasion, and Manchester's attitude to events was particularly interesting. For most of the war the Mancunians were mainly Parliamentarian but when the monarchy was restored they cheered the loudest. They obviously thought that Cromwell's lot were a bit on the dour side; after all, they did close the pubs, ban horse racing and forbade the celebration of Christmas.

1688: This was the year of what is generally referred to as the Glorious Revolution, when James II was removed (he was too Catholic in his views for many people) and replaced by William of Orange and his queen, Mary. But Lancashire had many Jacobite supporters and they resented having their legal monarch usurped by a ruler who was both Protestant and foreign. Resentment, in Lancashire, gathered pace.

1694: The trial took place of the so-called 'Lancashire Plotters'. These were all members of the Lancashire nobility who were accused of plotting to kill William and put James II back on the throne. They included Sir Thomas Clifton, Sir Roland Stanley, Philip Langton, William Dicconson, William Blundell and Lord Molyneux. Fortunately for them the evidence was rather flimsy and so they were acquitted, but it did not help Lord Molyneux. He was stripped of his position as Constable of Liverpool Castle, despite the 'not guilty' verdict.

1745: When the Young Pretender (better known as Bonny Prince Charlie) was brought back from exile in France the country found itself in the grip of rebellion once again. He raised an army of sympathisers in Scotland and marched south, hoping to pick up additional supporters on the way. But things did not go to plan and, after getting as far as Derby, he was forced to rethink his plans and head for home. One of the few places that did lend some support was Manchester, but the Manchester Regiment was unable to prevent the rout of Charlie's army. As it retreated, towns along the way, such as Preston and Lancaster, were plundered. In revenge, a Protestant mob in Liverpool vented their feelings by destroying a Catholic church.

1750: It was about this time that the greatest Revolution (the Industrial Revolution) began and Lancashire played a leading role in the social, agricultural and industrial changes which have so affected succeeding generations. Manchester acquired the soubriquet 'Cottonopolis' and symbolised the sudden and rapid industrialisation of the whole country in general, Lancashire in particular. Canals, railways, factories and mills mushroomed, and inventors such as Richard Arkwright (born in Preston) and James Hargreaves (born in Oswaltwistle) gave the world inventions which revolutionised many of the processes involved in the textile trades. The downside was that the advent of machines put a lot of agricultural labourers out of work or drove them off the land and into the cities where they lived in hovels and became slaves to the very machines they were supposed to be operating. The poor housing generated by the factories' need for cheap labour became the slums of the nineteenth and twentieth centuries. The factory and mill owners became rich as they churned out textiles and manufactured goods, but the workers who sweated from dawn till dusk suffered from disease, hunger and overcrowding.

1819: On 16 August of this year, an event took place in Manchester which has to be one of the worst examples of

crowd control in British history. Crowds had gathered to protest against dreadful working conditions, appalling housing, lack of representation in Parliament and unemployment. Contemporary reports suggest that the crowd was orderly and disciplined and that even something of a holiday atmosphere prevailed. By the time the crowd had reached Peter's Field (roughly where the Central Library now stands), the local yeomanry, who had been called out to maintain the peace, took fright at the sight of such a large crowd. They drew their sabres and charged, slashing left and right, straight into the mass of people. Fifteen people were killed and many more were injured. Politicians were horrified at what had happened and, so it is thought, hastened to bring about reform so that the massacre should never be repeated. The term by which the event is generally known is the Peterloo Massacre; an ironic reference to the glorious victory over Napoleon at Waterloo just four years before.

1830: Stephenson's Rocket won the competition to find the world's first viable railway locomotive at Rainhill. In the same year, the world's first inter-city passenger train service began operating between Liverpool and Manchester. The ceremonial inaugural celebrations were marred when the train ran over William Huskisson, who was both ex-President of the Board of Trade and MP for Liverpool, inflicting injuries from which he died a few hours later. It was a terrible tragedy but one that was not allowed to interfere with industrial progress, and the railways evolved to become one of the driving forces of Lancashire's industrial expansion.

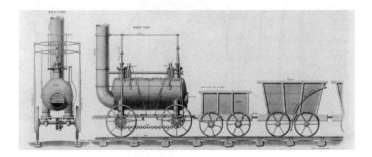

1838: The Anti-Corn Law League was formed in Manchester by businessmen who saw the Corn Laws as an impediment to free trade. The Corn Laws had been introduced in 1815 to deal with the economic crisis resulting from plummeting market prices for corn. It was hoped that by imposing prohibitively high import duties on foreign corn, British farmers would be able to make a living wage. But the whole policy was seen as protecting the landed gentry more than the farm worker and, also, the very concept was contrary to all notions of free trade. One of the leading lights in the Anti-Corn Law League was John Bright who was born in Rochdale.

1842: The ghosts of the Peterloo Massacre in Manchester reappeared in Preston on 13 August, when a group of cotton-mill workers found themselves in a similar situation to that of the earlier protesters. This time the workers assembled in Lune Street to protest against the mill owners' decision to cut their wages. They were confronted by the 72nd Highlanders who opened fire and killed five of the strikers,with many others wounded.

1844: Rochdale had strong associations with another social development, the foundation of the Co-operative movement. It grew out of a small group of men with strong social consciences who called themselves the Equitable Pioneers of Rochdale and who simply wanted to give people a fair deal when it came to buying the food they needed to feed their families. The basic idea was to form a club whose members would be guaranteed the opportunity of buying decent food for a reasonable price and, at the same time, to have a share of the profits which became known as the dividend.

1844/45: Parts of Lancashire were affected by events across the Irish Sea. The crop disease known as 'potato blight' virtually destroyed the vegetable, which formed a staple part of diet, before it was even dug out of the ground. Hunger stalked the land and many Irish families were faced with a choice: emigrate or die. Thousands fled to America, but thousands also settled in southern Lancashire and in particular in Liverpool. What was already a serious housing problem soon became a planning nightmare. People lived crowded together in unsanitary conditions and the result was inevitable: hundreds died of dysentery, and the crypt of St Anthony's Church on Scotland Road is still the last resting place of many of the famine's victims.

1853/54: In Preston, the mill owners still had not got the message that the workers were entitled to a living wage. This time when the mill workers demanded a reasonable wage, the owners' reply was the 'Great Lockout' when they closed all the factories and attempted to starve the workers and their families until they agreed to return to work with no increase in pay. Karl Marx saw these events as harbingers of revolution and called Preston the English St Petersburg.

1858: As the Industrial Revolution in Lancashire gathered pace more and more factories and mills came to rely on the power of steam. The only problem (or rather the main problem) was that steam boilers had a tendency to blow up if the operator failed to keep a watchful eye on the pressure gauge; the results could be catastrophic and/or fatal. In June 1858 this is exactly what happened at the Dean Mill in Rossendale when a boiler exploded like a bomb and killed three people who happened to be in the vicinity. In the same month, this time in Blackburn, another boiler exploded in a weaving shed, killing engineer Henry Seed. The blast was so powerful that it demolished a wall of the mill and caused some damage to three nearby cottages. Unfortunately, these were not isolated incidents. The history of nineteenth-century Lancashire is punctuated with accidents very similar to these. But they were frequently regarded as little more than the acceptable hazards which were all part of certain industrial occupations.

1903: Emmeline Pankhurst (and her daughters Sylvia and Christabel) from Manchester decided that it was time that the women of Britain had the right to vote. To begin with they tried gentle persuasion but soon discovered that this tactic was not going to bring the desired results, so they embarked on a campaign of increasing violence. At first, they simply heckled prominent politicians at meetings but when the government still refused to grant women the vote they adopted a more aggressive stance – they smashed shop windows and even set fire to Lloyd George's house. The Suffragettes, as the Pankhursts and their supporters were known, did not achieve their objective until 1918.

1914–18: Lancashire suffered, as did the rest of the country, from the terrible events that shook the whole of Europe in the First World War. The initial jingoism displayed by the crowds as they watched their sons, husbands and sweethearts marching off to war soon faded and was replaced by grief and broken hearts as news of the dead and mutilated filtered back home. Obviously, the Lancashire cotton mills found themselves swamped beneath orders for bandages, swabs and field dressings of all sorts.

1919–20: On the other hand, the war meant that many of the overseas markets were lost. There was a brief revival in 1919–20, but the heyday was over and even the most optimistic industrialists realised that there were grim times ahead for the Lancashire cotton industry.

1929: The Wall Street Crash in America plunged the world into an economic slump from which it took years to recover. Unemployment hit Lancashire hard as industry ground almost to a complete standstill. State aid for the unemployed was pitiful, and the daily grind became just one long struggle for survival.

1940: Lancashire was at war again, but this time the fighting was not all in a distant theatre of war; it was close to home, and cities such as Liverpool and Manchester suffered sustained bombing attacks designed to reduce the country to its knees. What tends to be forgotten, however, is that rural Lancashire suffered its share of nightmare bombing also. For security reasons the government of the day wanted to preserve the myth that Lancashire was a safe haven, untouched by the horrors of Luftwaffe bombing raids. The reality, however, was somewhat different and places such as Accrington, Clayton-le-Moors, Oswaldtwistle, Blackburn, Darwen, Whalley and several other unlikely targets had a bomb or bombs land in their midst. These incidents were nothing like what was happening in the industrial and commercial centres, but they were frightening enough at the time for the people concerned.

1944: On 23 August the little Lancashire town of Freckleton suffered a dreadful accident of war. An American Liberator bomber, based at Warton airfield, took off at 10.30 in the morning on what has been described as a test flight. The meteorological conditions were atrocious and the pilot, after a vain struggle with a storm over the Irish Sea, decided to return to base. But by the time he was approaching Freckleton the plane was almost out of control and it came in too low; its wing tip sliced through the corner of a building and the plane hit the ground at a terrifying speed. Three houses were completely demolished, but the real tragedy was still to come; when the plane hit the ground it did not stop but careered into the infants' department of Freckleton Holy Trinity School. Thirty-eight children, two teachers and twenty-one civilians and service personnel were killed.

Around 1950: A huge rebuilding programme now started in Lancashire. The war had seen thousands of houses and commercial buildings destroyed and they all had to be replaced, but it was only in the early 1950s that the finances could be found to begin the massive project. Furthermore, it was not only war-damaged properties that were to be replaced; the government of the day also saw it as an opportunity to get rid, once and for all, of many of the slum dwellings in places such as Liverpool, Salford, Preston and Manchester. The progress was painfully slow and as late as the '60s, many people, were still living in what now would be considered sub-standard housing. The downside of the rebuilding programme, however, was that the ill-advised politicians frequently listened to planners who favoured high-rise, high-density housing which did not go down well with the people who had to live in the new apartment blocks that had sprouted up everywhere. People found themselves scattered to the outlying new estates, where friends and neighbours could no longer keep in touch as they had done in the pre-war days. The communities were destroyed and often the community spirit was destroyed along with them.

1956: The Clean Air Act was passed and Lancashire, within a few years, was transformed. Until 1956 the commonest source of heat in homes was the open coal fire. They were lovely to see as you walked into a house on a foggy November night, but they were extremely inefficient and positively hazardous to health. They represented an ever-present fire hazard but also produced clouds of dense smoke which drifted into the atmosphere. Additionally, under certain conditions, and particularly in November and December, the smoke would combine with mists and fogs to produce a noxious combination known as smog ('smoke' and 'fog'), which caused many deaths, particularly in the industrial towns of the north, including Lancashire.

1957–59: Liverpool lost two iconic modes of transport. The Overhead Railway, which had run from Garston to Seaforth for sixty years, was dismantled. Its metal framework had begun to disintegrate and it was now considered too dangerous to operate and too expensive to repair. At the same time, the last tram completed its final journey, and the clanking and screeching noises which had been a backdrop to so many people's lives in Liverpool suddenly stopped. Now the dominant background noise in the port's main roads was that produced by cars and buses.

Around 1962: All of a sudden, in what seems like an unexpected and totally inexplicable explosion of creativity, Liverpool became the centre of the entertainments universe. Gerry and the Pacemakers, The Beatles, Cilla Black and about 300 other groups and singers took not just the country but the whole world by storm. They provided a much needed fillip to post-war Britain and their record sales brought in millions to swell the Exchequer's coffers.

1974: For reasons best known to themselves, the Tory government decided that Lancashire's ancient borders needed to be re-drawn. The large conurbations of Liverpool and Manchester, in addition to the smaller towns such as Southport, found themselves no longer part of Lancashire. Of course, there were protests and, of course, they were totally ignored. The ancient county lost huge swathes of territory and thousands of Lancastrians went to bed one night and woke up the next morning as Merseysiders, Greater Mancunians and Seftonians etc.

1984: The coal miners of Britain found themselves on a collision course with the government, particularly the prime minister Mrs Margaret Thatcher. Lancashire was hit hard and St Helens, with its Bold, Sutton Manor and Parkside pits, was on the front line in the miners' confrontation with the authorities. A series of mini civil wars broke out: the miners fought the police, and miner fought miner over the question of whether to strike or not. Fathers, sons, and brothers found themselves on different sides of the picket line. When the strikers finally gave way and returned to work, the death knell had been sounded for coal mining as a major industry in Britain.

2008: Liverpool was now the Capital of Culture, and Phil Redmond was appointed Creative Director. It turned out to be just the medicine the city needed after being in the economic sick-bay for so long, and when the year came to an end there were few people who thought that Liverpool's hosting of the event was anything less than an astounding success.

AND A BIT OF TRIVIA

The numbering system around the modern dart board was devised by one Brian Gamlin, a carpenter from Bury, in 1896.

The world's first test-tube baby was born in Oldham in 1978.

The town of Marsden in Lancashire changed its name to Nelson in 1805, in memory of Admiral Nelson who was killed at the Battle of Trafalgar.

LORD NELSON.

3

OUT AND ABOUT

Driving through Lancashire you might suddenly find yourself stepping back in time and admiring the unchanging scenery as you pass through pretty little villages with quaint-sounding names such as Chipping and Claughton-on-Brock, or faintly foreign-sounding ones such as Poulton-le-Fylde, Grimsargh or Goosnargh. And when you start to see signposts for places such as Tockholes, Ramsbottom and Oswaldtwistle you know you are in a county which is pretty much unlike any other.

SOME BASIC FACTS AND STATS

The county we now think of as historic Lancashire was formed from the old Saxon administrative districts based on manorial lands. These were known as hundreds (which were subdivided into parishes) of which there were six when the Normans arrived: Amounderness, Blackburn, Leyland, Lonsdale, Salford and West Derby.

In 1974 the boundary changes meant that parts of the territory became part of new Cumbria and, in the south, many old Lancastrian towns were absorbed into the new administrative districts such as Greater Manchester, Merseyside and Sefton. Warrington became part of Cheshire, but Lancashire gained an area around Clitheroe which had formerly been part of the West Riding of Yorkshire.

The shire county is now divided into the districts of Burnley, Chorley, Fylde, Hyndburn, Lancaster, West Lancashire, Wyre, Pendle, Preston, Ribble Valley, Rossendale and South Ribble.

Area (post 1974): 1,189 sq. miles
Population: just under 1.5 million (2011)
County Town: Lancaster
Administrative Centre: Preston
Main rivers: Ribble, Mersey, Lune, Irwell, Douglas, Wyre, Calder, Darwen, Kent.

Despite the high-density population and urban sprawl in certain areas, Lancashire is still classed as being 80 per cent rural.

AROUND THE DISTRICTS

Blackpool
Population: 142,000 approx. (2011)
Place name origin: The modern town takes its name from the nearby dark peaty lake or pool, which was filled in and built on in the nineteenth century. Although the pool has now gone, its ancient name of Blacke-Poole survives in a more modern form.

Little more than a coastal hamlet until the mid-eighteenth century, when it was 'discovered' by those who indulged in the new craze of sea bathing (believing it was good for the health), Blackpool suddenly found itself the destination for thousands of people who just fancied a bit of a break from the daily grind. In 1781, as Blackpool's 7 miles of sandy beaches proved just too strong a magnet for northern sun worshippers, stage coaches began bringing people in from places as far afield as Manchester and Halifax. But when the trains arrived in the 1840s, Blackpool experienced a kind of Klondike gold rush. All of a sudden the tiny hamlet had to cope with hordes of holiday makers and hotels, theatres, pubs, tea-rooms and boarding houses began to mushroom. The foundations of the poor man's Las Vegas were

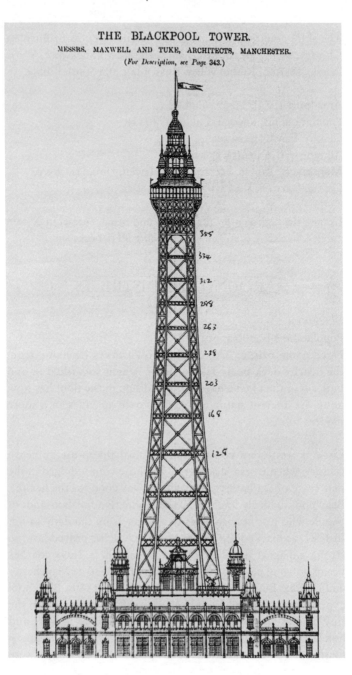

THE BLACKPOOL TOWER.
MESSRS. MAXWELL AND TUKE, ARCHITECTS, MANCHESTER.
(*For Description, see Page 343.*)

lain as keen-eyed entrepreneurs spotted a golden opportunity to cash in on the economic boom that engulfed the whole area.

When Blackpool Tower opened in 1894 it acquired a symbolic significance almost overnight. Modelled on the Eiffel Tower in Paris and, at 518ft, it dominated the skyline and came to symbolise cheap, 'kiss-me-quick' hats and Blackpool-rock holidays for those who could not afford the more expensive kind on offer in more refined parts of the country.

Next to the Tower, the most famous of Blackpool's attractions have to be the trams, which began service in 1885 and have been running ever since. Far from being just a functional form of transport for the town's inhabitants, the trams are a definite tourist attraction, especially in autumn when they are lit up as an integral part of the annual 'light-fest' known as the Blackpool Illuminations.

During the Second World War, Blackpool was virtually unscathed and it has been suggested that this was on the direct orders of Adolf Hitler. He is thought to have wanted to preserve the town as a place for 'rest and recuperation' for his troops after the invasion and occupation of the whole country. Also in the Second World War, the Polish Air Force in Exile had its HQ in Talbot Square.

Some notable people associated with Blackpool include Brian London (boxer), Janet Munro (actress), Ricky Tomlinson (actor), Syd Little (comedian) and Alistaire Cooke (journalist and broadcaster).

Accrington
Population: 35,200 approx. (2001)
River: Hyndburn
Place name origin: From the Anglo-Saxon *aecer* 'acorn' and *tun* 'farmstead or village'. The original settlement stood on the edge of the Rossendale Forest and could well have been the centre of a pig-rearing community.

Until about 1830 Accrington was classed as a largish village. However, the Industrial Revolution was to have a tremendous effect on the whole area. The plentiful supply of water from the surrounding rivers and streams meant that it was an ideal place to set up mills and factories. Once these mills became established, the usual thing happened: the owners did not wish to live near the noisy, filthy mills that provided their wealth, so they built substantial dwellings on the outer reaches of the town. On the other hand, the workers had to live within walking distance of the spinning sheds and weaving mills and as a result a certain dichotomy of income divided the town.

Nevertheless, the workers were not entirely docile, and Accrington's history is punctuated with industrial unrest, just like most of the Lancashire mill towns. On one occasion in 1830, in what came to be known as the 'plug riots', the mill workers, many of whom had been made redundant, smashed the plugs off the machinery that drove the looms and other technical wizardry. The water and steam gushed out, the machinery came to a standstill and the mills were forced to close. But, as with many such protests in Lancashire in the nineteenth century, the action was short-lived and the mills soon reopened. In 1860, however, the owners and workers alike faced a crisis from the other side of the Atlantic. The American Civil War caused a cotton famine in Lancashire and the whole county, including Accrington, was badly affected.

A more modern industry in Accrington is brick manufacturing and one of the town's claims to fame is that it supplied most of the bricks (which have a reputation for being extremely hard) with which the Empire State Building in New York was built.

Some famous people born in Accrington include Harrison Birtwistle (composer), Julie Hesmondhalgh and Vicky Entwistle (both *Coronation Street* actors), and Jeanette Winterson (author).

Preston

Population: 114,000 approx. (2008)
River: Ribble
Place name origin: Anglo-Saxon *preosta* 'priest' and *tun* 'farmstead' or 'village'.

As the origin of the name suggests, there was a large religious community here at one time and evidence of this survives in one of the city's main thoroughfares, Friargate. Preston was granted its charter in 1179 (when Liverpool was just a collection of fishermen's huts), which meant that its population had certain rights, including the right to hold fairs and markets.

The Franciscan friars arrived in 1260 but their friary was closed down by Henry VIII in 1539 as part of his religious 'reorganisation' of the country. Yet despite Henry's dispute with the Pope, Preston remained mainly Roman Catholic and there is still a large Catholic element in the population today.

The damp climate and the town's easy access to the sea made it an ideal place for the textile industry. In the early days, wool and linen formed the basis of industry in the town but, by the mid- to late-eighteenth century, the production of cotton had taken over as the main industry. In 1771 the first cotton mill opened and this marked the start of what was to be a thriving industry (with one or two hiccups) until just after the First World War. Unemployment now ran high, until the new industries such as those based on the production of electrical goods and engineering were firmly established. Car production began in Leyland in 1907, and aircraft construction in Preston in 1918. Then, when Courtaulds opened a rayon factory in the area in 1939 it seemed as though Preston's industrial future was secure. Much of Preston's industrial success was reflected in the magnificence of some of its public buildings: the Harris Museum and Art Gallery was opened in 1893, and the Sessions House was built in 1903. This was then extended to include the Town Hall in 1933. Then, in 1992, the ancient town became a centre of learning when the old Lancashire Polytechnic became a fully fledged university known as UCLAN (University of Central Lancashire). In 2001 a football museum was opened in the town, one of the last civic events before Preston became a city in 2002.

Some famous Prestonians include Nick Park CBE (artist and film producer), Eddie Calvert (musician known as 'the man with the golden trumpet'), Roy Barraclough MBE (actor), John Inman (actor), and Sir Tom Finney (footballer).

Liverpool

Population: 470,000 approx. (2011)

River: Mersey

Place name origin: either from Anglo-Saxon *lifer* 'liver' and *pul* 'pool' meaning 'muddy water' or Norse *hlith* 'slope' and *pul* meaning 'slope by the pool'.

In 1207, King John decided that the little hamlet in the north-west of his kingdom would become a port from which he could send his armies over to Ireland. He planned the original street layout, which can still be seen today, but could not have foreseen how his creation would grow and become the virtual powerhouse of the nation. By the seventeenth and eighteenth centuries Liverpool was the country's lifeline with the rest of the world and, as England became one of the wealthiest nations on earth, Liverpool became one of the wealthiest towns (it only became a city in 1880) in the country, if not the world. Industry and commerce just grew and grew in and around Liverpool, and the town expanded over the centuries to accommodate the influx of people from all over the world who wanted to settle there. Hence there is hardly a native Liverpudlian (or Scouser) who cannot trace his origins back to Irish, Scottish, Welsh, Chinese, African, Jewish, German, French or Polish roots (and I have probably missed a few!). The result is a city which is unique in the whole of Britain: its accent is like no other; its natives enjoy a sense of humour unequalled anywhere else; its architecture is among the finest in the world; and the genetic mixing bowl has produced talented people in every sport, in the arts, in science and in medicine. In fact, there is hardly any human activity in which Liverpudlians have not played an active role.

Famous people associated with Liverpool include the Beatles (singers), Ken Dodd (comedian and singer), Rex Harrison (actor),

Beryl Bainbridge (author), William Gladstone (politician), and Wayne Rooney (footballer).

Southport
Population: 90,400 approx. (2001)
Place name origin: A modern name first attributed in 1798.

Until the eighteenth century there was hardly any habitation here at all, although the names of surrounding hamlets and villages suggest that such habitation as there was began with the arrival of early settlers from Scandinavia (Birkdale, Scarisbrick, North Meols etc.). But it would appear that a minor population explosion occurred around the twelfth century, when a primitive place of worship was built on the site of what is now St Cuthbert's Church in the heart of the delightfully quaint Churchtown, on the edge of modern Southport.

In fact, the town we know think of as Southport, with its elegant Lord Street (claimed by some to have been modelled on the Champs Elysées in Paris), owed its foundation to a resident of Churchtown and might never have come into existence had he not had a bit of a brainwave. In 1792, William Sutton, the landlord of the only inn in the village (then the Black Bull, now the Hesketh Arms), built himself a little house in the sand dunes on the coast, which he could use when he fancied going for a swim in the Irish Sea. A few years later, in 1798, a woman from Wigan also decided to do a spot of building in the area. She built a house which she then turned into a sort of latter-day 'holiday let', which no doubt provided her with a tidy income. Not to be outdone, William Sutton then decided to increase his investment in the area and built another inn, which he called the South Port Hotel. Within a few years, the town had begun to expand at a rapid rate (the arrival of the railways saw to that) and building development took off. Mr Sutton's hotel disappeared but the name remained and the whole area came to be known as South Port. The two words eventually merged into one and the town of Southport was here to stay. But the question does remain: why should a seaside town on the north-west coast of England be called South Port when it is neither in the south nor a port?

One suggestion is that William Sutton and the lady from Wigan founded their businesses to the 'south' of Churchtown, where William already had a pub, and the 'port' element is simply an archaic use of the word denoting any trading place, whether it be inland or on the coast.

Today, of course, Southport is known as a rather smart place to live (the footballers and WAGs who have bought houses there testify to that), and the Royal Birkdale Golf Course brings in thousands of tourists every year. Added to this there is the annual Southport flower show which many consider a worthy rival to its southern counterpart in Chelsea.

Notable people who were either born or chose to live in Southport include Frank Hampson (artist and creator of *Dan Dare*), Revd Marcus Morris (founder of the *Eagle* comic), Anthony Quayle (actor), A.J.P Taylor (historian), Jean Alexander (former *Coronation Street* and *Last of the Summer Wine* actress), and Lee Mack (comedian).

Did you know that ...

People from Southport are known locally as 'sandgrounders'?

Prior to becoming President of France, Louis-Napoléon Bonaparte lived on Lord Street from 1846–1848?

St Cuthbert is the patron saint of the North of England, sailors and shepherds?

Morecambe

Population: 39,000 approx. (2001)
Place name origin: Adapted from the name Morikambe, given to the place by the second-century geographer Ptolemy.

Morecambe is another one of those coastal towns which developed into a seaside resort in the nineteenth century after the development of the railroads. Until then, this quiet little fishing village was known as Poulton-le-Sands ('the settlement by the pool near the sands'). When tourism began to flourish in the area it was actually Morecambe Bay that was the main attraction and it was only later, when Poulton-le-Sands was swallowed up by the burgeoning hotels and cafés, that it was decided to adopt the name Morecambe for the whole area. There are probably three things that make Morecambe famous. Firstly, Morecambe Bay potted shrimps, a local delicacy which disappeared from our fishmongers' shops a while ago but has recently enjoyed a resurgence of popularity. Then the treacherous quicksands and tidal bore which can trap the unwary and have been known in the past to lead to tragedy. Visitors are warned not to venture out onto the sands alone, no matter how beautiful and enchanting they can appear. Trained local guides conduct tours for the curious but ignorant, as experience has taught them how to 'read' the sands and where and when it is safe to venture out and when it definitely is not. Then, of course, there is Morecambe's third claim to fame: Eric Morecambe. He entertained theatre and television audiences from the 1960s till his sudden and untimely death in 1984. He was born in the town and is commemorated with a statue in his likeness, created by the sculptor Graham Ibbeson, which now graces the promenade.

And did you know that …

The football team, Morecambe FC, are known locally as 'the shrimps'?

The Miss Great Britain beauty contest was held there from 1956 to 1989?

The RNLI based its very first life-saving hovercraft in Morecambe? It became operational in 2002.

Bury

Population: 61,000 approx. (2012)
River: Irwell
Place name origin: From the Anglo-Saxon *burh* meaning stronghold or fort.

The town grew up around a market which started trading as far back as 1440, but there is evidence of human activity in the area from as early as Roman times. Like many other areas within Lancashire its real period of growth dates from the Industrial Revolution, when its position on the banks of the River Irwell meant that it was ideally suited for the textile industry. When the calico printing factory opened in 1773, it was a signal that the town was going to be a major player in the industrial life of the north of England. The calico printing works was the brainchild of the Peels, the same family that produced one of the country's most successful prime ministers.

Redevelopment, changes in consumer preferences and better housing have all contributed to the changing cityscape that Bury has experienced over recent years. Most of the cramped, insanitary housing of the eighteenth and nineteenth centuries has disappeared, and there is now little evidence that the town once relied on the textile industry for its livelihood. Nonetheless, the market around which the town grew all those years ago still thrives … and what a market it is! It has 370 stalls and a food and fish hall, and endless lines of stalls selling just about anything a shopper could need. The pride and joy of the whole establishment, however, are the stalls specialising in traditional Lancashire fare such as tripe and black pudding. And the proud boast of those who sell it is that Bury black pudding is the best in the world.

Some famous people from Bury include Sir Robert Peel (Prime Minister), John Kay (inventor), Richmal Crompton (author), Helen Flanagan (*Coronation Street* actress), Gary Neville (footballer), Danny Boyle (film producer), Lisa Riley (TV personality), and Cherie Blair (wife of Tony Blair, former Prime Minister).

Rochdale
Population: 46,000 approx. (2001)
River: Roch

There is some confusion over the origin of the name Rochdale. The temptation is to think that the town takes its name from the river on which it stands, but this is not so.

The river used to be called the Rached; this took its name from an earlier settlement which appeared in written evidence from the twelfth century as Rachedham. In the Domesday Book it was recorded as Recedham, thought to be from the Anglo-Saxon *reced* meaning a 'hall' or 'manor house'.

Rochdale, as the settlement eventually came to be known, received its Royal Charter in 1251 and was soon to blossom into one of the most important centres of the wool trade in the north of England. By the nineteenth century it was well and truly established as the centre of the whole textile industry and then, when the Rochdale Canal opened in 1804, the sky was the limit. Textiles produced in the town now had easy access to Yorkshire, Manchester and from there to all the major towns and cities in the country.

Like most of the Lancashire mill towns, Rochdale's architecture offers a stunning contrast in styles and taste. There are the usual terraced houses where the mill workers lived (although these are now disappearing fast), as well as municipal and church buildings of astounding beauty – the Gothic Revival Town Hall is one of the finest of its kind in the country. Nikolaus Pevsner, the architectural historian, was full of praise for the building and it is believed that Adolf Hitler was also a passionate admirer. In fact, he is thought to have given instructions that, after England's expected capitulation, Rochdale Town Hall was to be dismantled brick by brick and transported back to somewhere in Germany, where it was to be rebuilt.

St Chad's parish church is another building of note in the town. The church we can see in all its splendour today is not all that old. It was built by the Victorians but records tell us that there was a church on the site before 1170 and there is a distinct possibility that a place of worship existed on the same site in Saxon times.

Some notable people born in Rochadale include Bill Oddie (TV personality), Gracie Fields (singer), and Anna Friel (actress).

Did you know that...

The Romantic poet Lord Byron was styled Lord Byron of Rochdale?

St Chad is claimed to be the patron saint of healing springs and wells? He is also, since the botched elections in the United States in 2000, and somewhat in jest, claimed by some to be the patron saint of disputed elections.

Manchester
Population: 503,000 approx. (2011)
River: Irwell
Place name origin: From the Latin *Mamucium*.

'Cottonopolis', 'Warehouse city', 'Rainy City', 'Madchester' and 'Mancunia' are just some of the nicknames which this magnificent city has acquired over the years. The Roman name,

from which the modern name is derived, was something of a borrowing itself, from the Celtic description of the land on which the original settlement seems to have been built. Most linguistic authorities now agree that the Celtic root of the original name was *mamme* meaning 'breast' – presumably because the fort or forts which formed the nucleus of the pre-historic settlement were on a hill (now the site of Manchester Cathedral) which they thought resembled a human breast. If this is the true origin of the name (and it seems safe to assume that it is) it provides a fitting metaphor; Manchester has given birth to and nurtured industrialists, businessmen and women, scientists, artists, writers, sportsmen and women, architects, and a host of other people outstanding in their field. The university (which grew out of Owens College) is second to none; Ernest Rutherford, who discovered the structure of the atom, and Alan Turing, who pioneered the work which gave us the modern computer, both had their laboratories at Manchester University.

We can argue that Manchester as we know it today came into being on the orders of the Roman general Agricola who, in AD 79, ordered the construction of a garrison in the area as a defensive bulwark against the marauding Celtic tribes who were a constant threat to the Roman interests around the towns we now know as Chester and York. But it was in the Middle Ages that Manchester experienced an explosion of development: Flemish weavers came over from the Continent and, as was the case in so many northern towns, they used their skills and know-how to lay the basis for a textile industry which thrived and grew over the centuries.

During the Industrial Revolution, Manchester's expansion continued apace and the city came to play a crucial role not only in the economic growth of the nation but in its social history as well. Industrialists and businessmen were creating vast wealth for the country as a whole (and for themselves!) but the social cost was high; the workers at the bottom of the economic pile endured dreadful conditions and writers such as Dickens, Mrs Gaskell and Friedrich Engels (who was a mill owner himself) wrote about the plight of the many who toiled for the benefit of the few.

Famous people who hail from Manchester include Liam Gallaher (singer), Harold Lever (politician), Wes Brown (footballer) and Arthur Delaney (artist).

Did you know that ...

The first bus service in Britain ran from Pendleton to Manchester and was opened in 1824? It was basically just a horse and cart with several seats in it, but it picked up passengers and dropped them off at various stops on the way, so can claim to have been the first omnibus.

The newspaper we all know as the *Guardian* began life as the *Manchester Guardian* in 1821? It dropped 'Manchester' from its title in 1959.

Lancaster
Population: 50,000 approx. (2001)
River: Lune
Place name origin: *lon*, a Celtic word meaning 'health'.

In the Domesday Book Lancaster was referred to as 'Lonecaestre' and this was derived from the Celtic *lon* and *castrum*, the Latin for a 'camp'. It is generally assumed by linguists that the reason the Celtic people of the region (the Brigantes) used their word for 'health' was that they believed that the pure water of the river had a beneficial effect on the wellbeing of those who drank from it or bathed in it. The same linguistic root can still be heard today when an Irishman or Scotsman raises his tot of whiskey or whisky.

The Romans built a fortress on the banks of the River Lune as part of their defences in one of the most northerly outposts of their empire. When they left in the fifth century, the Vikings and Saxons arrived but it was not until the years following the Norman Conquest of 1066 that development of the area really began. William I had an uneasy time of it for a few years whilst he attempted to quell the northern provinces and build the virtually impenetrable stone castles which formed part of his military tactics. The ancient Roman stockade became the site of a massive new structure which dominates the area even today and which we now know as Lancaster Castle. The keep

Did you know that ...

The title Duke of Lancaster does not take account of the gender of the office-holder and so Queen Elizabeth II, the present incumbent, is referred to as the Duke of Lancaster?

Traditionally, the National Anthem was slightly altered in Lancashire to include the lines 'God save our gracious Queen, long live our noble Duke ...'?

was added later, in the twelfth century, and King John finished the job by adding the walls and a sizeable gateway.

From the Middle Ages onwards, Lancaster's history did not really mirror that of the rest of the country. Its northerly position meant that it suffered from incursions by the marauding Scots, and it was struck by the plague several times in the sixteenth century. But that is really where the similarity ends: the small port was soon overshadowed by its larger southern neighbour, Liverpool, and the boom in textiles and coalmining in the areas around Preston and Manchester never really happened in Lancaster. The production of oilcloth and linoleum became the mainstay of industrial production in the mid-nineteenth century and this was supported by furniture production here which lasted till 1962. Nowadays the industries which make a major contribution to Lancaster's economy are those associated with Information Technology and electronics, although tourism also plays an important role. Nor must we forget the contribution to the local economy played by the University of Lancaster which was opened in 1964.

Famous people from Lancaster include Andy Wear (actor), Lawrence Binyon (poet), Steve Kemp (musician), and John McGuinness (motor cyclist and TT race legend).

Salford
Population: 73,000 approx. (2001)
River: Irwell
Place name origin: From the Anglo-Saxon *sealhford* meaning the ford where the willows grow. Ultimately it is derived from the Latin *salix* meaning 'willow'.

Until the Industrial Revolution, Salford was more important from both a commercial and a cultural point of view than its neighbour Manchester. The Industrial Revolution did not create Salford's industrial importance, it merely enhanced it. The textile industry was well established in Salford by the eighteenth and nineteenth centuries and indeed had been a flourishing concern since the fourteenth, but then it traded mainly in wool and fustian. Cottage industries also thrived and helped lay the basis for Salford's wealth with shoe manufacturing, brewing and clog making all playing their part. When the Industrial Revolution arrived, it transformed Manchester into an industrial giant but Salford's star began to wane and the main cause for this can, arguably, be summed up in one word: water. The mills that grew up around Manchester did so largely because the Irwell

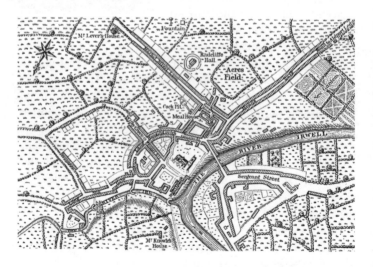

flows faster there and was more suited to driving the large mill machines. Salford's gently meandering, almost motionless waters were deemed too gentle in the new age – powerful machinery needs a powerful water flow to drive it.

Salford developed from an old Saxon Manor (it was at the centre of one of the hundreds that eventually formed the basis of the county of Lancashire) and was granted its first charter by the Earl of Chester in 1230. This gave it the status of a free borough with certain distinct commercial advantages and so Salford became a mercantile magnet as well as a very attractive place to live. Some very influential people moved into the area and not only established businesses but set up home there as well. However, the rich merchants were not happy to live in the hovels that the ordinary folk lived in; they wanted something much grander and could afford to build substantial properties, some of which still survive today. In the late Middle Ages, the area around Salford was already being described as a place 'rich in its manor houses'.

When the Industrial Revolution exploded, the resulting Salford was definitely two-sided: industry, now based largely on cotton, thrived, but the need for factory and mill workers generated overcrowded living conditions on a previously unknown scale. This in turn spawned economic and social problems which proved virtually insoluble until the 1960s. Even then the difficulties were not eradicated totally and the city is still grappling with them today.

Did you know that...

Salford is thought to be the very first city in England which offered its citizens a completely free public lending library?

It is also claimed to be home to the first street in the world to enjoy the benefits of gas lighting? This was installed in Chapel Street in 1806.

Clitheroe
Population: 15,000 approx. (2001)
Place name origin: From the Celtic *clyder* or *clither* meaning 'a heap of [loose] stones', and the Anglo-Saxon *hoh* meaning a 'hill'. So the original settlement was known as 'the hill with loose stones'.

An ancient Saxon town in the lee of Pendle Hill, Clitheroe was recorded in 1102 as Cliderhou and grew up around what we now know as the smallest Norman castle in England, which also happens to be one of the oldest extant buildings in Lancashire. Clitheroe was granted a charter in 1283 by Henry de Lacy, confirming its right to hold markets and fairs which had originally been granted to the town in the twelfth century.

In more recent times, Clitheroe was the unlikely venue for one of the most momentous and fateful meetings in the history of aviation, and the area of the town around Whittle Close is a pretty good clue as to the reason why. In 1942 a group of aeronautical engineers from the Rolls-Royce and Rover companies met in the Swan and Royal Hotel to talk about the possibilities of a major development in aircraft engine design. More specifically, they were in the hotel to have dinner and discuss the jet engine which

The African Queen

Most people would agree that one of the finest films to come out of Hollywood was *The African Queen*, starring Humphrey Bogart and Katharine Hepburn. But few of the film's many admirers probably realise that the little boat (the real star of the film) was built in Lancashire. Originally named The Livingstone she was built in 1912 at the Lytham Shipbuilding Yard and was used as a cargo boat for the British East Africa Rail Company. She had been chugging along the rivers in and around the Congo over forty years when the film's director, John Huston, spotted her and knew instinctively that she was just what he needed for the film.

The little boat is now a tourist attraction in the Florida Keys.

had originally been designed by the young RAF engineer Frank Whittle (later Air Commodore Sir Frank Whittle) as early as the 1930s. After dinner the representatives of the two companies shook hands signalling that the deal had been done and we all know what happened next – air travel got a lot faster and the world got a lot smaller.

A visitor to Clitheroe is in for a pleasant surprise, especially if he is a professional or amateur oenologist (a posh word for wine buff). Just a moderate leg-stretch from the castle is a world-class wine merchants shop and walking through the door is like entering another world. In an instant the visitor finds himself in a cavernous warren of cellars stocked (and stacked) with wines from all over the world, and he could be forgiven for thinking that he has stepped into *la cave* of a magnificent French château. Anyone with an interest in the pleasure of the vine could lose himself for hours browsing among the thousands of bottles on display at any one time.

SOME INTERESTING
PLACE NAMES IN LANCASHIRE

Fazakerley: Now just a suburb of Liverpool and known to local people as 'Fazak', we can be certain that there must have been a settlement here in ancient times, as the name is derived from the Anglo-Saxon *faes* 'edge', *aecer* 'field' and *leah* 'meadow', so the place must originally have been known as the 'meadow at the edge of the field'.

Crank: A little hamlet about four miles from Skelmersdale and situated in the midst of luscious farming country. It used to boast a number of pubs but now just has The Red Cat, much used by the local farming community. Although small, the hamlet used to enjoy its own little railway station, Crank Halt, but this closed to passengers in 1952 and then to freight in 1964.

Anglezarke: Situated in the Borough of Chorley, Anglezarke (population twenty-three) used to be a centre for hill-farming and some small-scale coal mining, but these industries are now long gone. The odd-looking name is a combination of Norse and Celtic: the first element is derived from *Anlaf*, a Scandinavian personal name, and *argh,* a Celtic dialect word meaning 'hill pasture', so, putting it all together, we see that the name originally informed us that the area was 'Anlaf's hill farm'. In AD 1200 the hamlet was known as *Andelevesarewe*, but by the 1550s this had become *Anlazarghe*.

In 1984, Anglezarke Quarry (now popular with rock climbers) featured in the TV series *Jewel in the Crown,* based on the *Raj Quartet* by Paul Scott.

Blacko: A pretty little hamlet on the border between Lancashire and Yorkshire, Blacko is thought to have originally been called Blackho, the 'ho' being a corruption of 'hill'. Why exactly the hill was described as black is the subject of some discussion, as it is no darker than any other hill in the area. There are those who say that on the original map (dating from 1580) it was

coloured black, as it was the subject of an unresolved dispute over land ownership.

Blacko has two claims to fame, both of which are associated with former residents. People old enough to remember the family listening radio shows of the 1950s will remember the 'vertically challenged' comedian Jimmy Clitheroe. The host of *The Clitheroe Kid*, he could be heard in just about every house in the land at eleven o'clock on a Sunday morning. He was born James Robinson in nearby Clitheroe but grew up in Blacko, where he attended the primary school in the 1920s.

It is also claimed that in the seventeenth century another resident, a certain Mary Towneley, left England and married Captain Augustine Warner, who had sailed off to seek his fortune as a settler in Virginia. One of their descendants was none other than George Washington, America's first president.

In 2011, Blacko won the competition to find Lancashire's 'Best Kept Village'.

Oswaldtwistle: If you try to pronounce the name of this place as it is written you will be in a minority of one! Just about everybody in Lancashire refers to it as 'Ozzel twizzle', and that's when they are being formal. Normally it is universally known as 'Ossy'. The first part of the name, Oswald, is simply an Anglo-Saxon personal name, but the second element is a little more interesting – 'twistle' is derived from the Anglo-Saxon word *twisla* meaning 'a fork in a river', so the name must at one time have designated a place where the river divided on or near a stretch of land belonging to, presumably, a Saxon landowner called Oswald. Who exactly this Oswald was nobody can say with any degree of certainty.

When the Industrial Revolution erupted, Ossy was at the centre of the action. The town provided men who worked in about two dozen mills and about the same number of coal mines. Most of these are now gone.

Probably the most famous historical personage to come from the area was James Hargreaves, who revolutionised the spinning industry by inventing the spinning jenny in the eighteenth century.

St Helens: Why should a town, situated in the heart of a heavily industrialised part of Lancashire (coal mining, glass manufacturing and important chemical industry used to dominate the area) be named after a saint? Until the nineteenth century this was a relatively sparsely populated part of the county and this is probably the clue to how the town acquired its name. There are references, written around 1550, to a 'chapel of ease' dedicated to St Elyn (later written as St Helen) in the area. Chapels of ease were erected to provide places of worship if the parish church was too far away for people to be expected to travel. So it would appear that the still thriving industrial town we know today owes its origins to the church authorities' concern for parishioners in outlying districts.

St Helen is the patron saint of archaeologists and divorced people.

Besses o' th' Barn: Originally a little hamlet in Whitefield (Bury) there is very little information available on the history of this quaintly named part of Lancashire. It does appear, however, that the area took its name from an eighteenth-century local

inn (with barn attached) run by a landlady called Bess. The inn was demolished sometime in the early 1900s but the name has remained, although only strangers refer to the area by its full name. Locals simply call it 'Besses'.

Bickerstaffe: A little village situated about five miles south of Ormskirk, its name is a pretty good clue to what must have been one of the main industries there in times gone by. It is derived from the Anglo-Saxon word *bicere* meaning 'beekeeper' and Scandinavian *staeth*, 'landing place'. The original settlement would have been a place where beekeepers landed or delivered their hives and/or honey.

Dunnockshaw: This charming little village situated just south of Burnley has a name which is a little problematic for linguists. The 'shaw' bit is no problem; it is derived from an Anglo-Saxon word *sceaga* meaning a 'small wood' or 'copse'. The 'Dunnoc' part however has never actually been found, but is thought to be a slightly later word than sceaga and meaning a 'hedge sparrow'. The consensus of opinion, therefore, is that the name probably designates a small wood or copse which was known to be frequented by hedge sparrows.

Chipping: This village has absolutely nothing to do with frying slices of potato or chopping little bits off a hunk of rock. In Anglo-Saxon it was *cēping* and simply meant 'market'. The word root is *cēap meaning* 'price', 'bargain' or 'commercial transaction', and other words connected with it include 'cheap' and 'chapman' (an old word for a trader). In a slightly varied form, it is also the origin of the expression 'to chop and change', which originally meant to buy and sell.

Eccles: Although some disagree, the majority of linguists believe that the name is derived from an ancient term denoting the presence of a Roman-British church by which the original settlement was known. The term 'Eccles' is derived ultimately from the Greek *ekklesia*, 'an assembly', as is the word 'ecclesiastic'.

4

HAUNTINGS, SUPERSTITIONS AND WITCHCRAFT

If you don't like 'ghosties and ghoulies and long legged beasties, and things that go bump in the night', stay out of Lancashire. Just about every nook and cranny, big city and tiny hamlet in the county has got its fair share of strange goings-on, weird happenings and distinctly odd characters. On the other hand, if you like to hear the kind of tale that makes the hairs on the back of your neck stand up, read on …

FAIRIES

Penwortham Woods (or what is left of them), on the outskirts of Preston, is the setting for a Lancashire legend dating back to the 1880s. The story goes that two men were strolling through the woods one beautiful moonlit night when they suddenly heard the sound of the bells of the nearby St Mary's Church ringing out. The next thing they saw stopped them in their tracks for there, right in front of them, was a procession of 'little people' (fairies) carrying a tiny coffin in which lay the corpse of a fairy. The two men had accidentally stumbled upon a Penwortham Fairy Funeral.

All this may or may not be true, but the fact that the two men had just left the Black Horse pub might have some bearing on the legend's validity.

BOGGARTS

Another type of fairy was the 'boggart' which could take almost any shape it wanted either male or female. In Lancashire they were quite numerous and seemed to delight in driving people mad with their mischievous and even malicious ways. In Longridge, just outside Preston, a tale is told of one of these alarming sprites who took on the form of a headless young woman who seemed to derive cruel enjoyment from startling people on dark nights. On one occasion, wearing a hood to conceal her headless state and carrying a heavy basket, she appeared to a young man wending his way to the White Bull pub. He, being of a considerate nature, offered to carry the basket for her and she welcomed his gesture of kindness. But then, as he was taking hold of the basket, he dropped it and out popped the 'young woman's' head, staring fixedly at the poor lad with huge bulging eyes. Understandably, he took fright and ran off as fast as he could, disappearing into the darkness. And as he ran all he could hear was the boggart's spine-chilling laughter.

The boggarts of old Lancashire were said to have a leader called 'Owd [old] Hob'.

In Lancashire it used to be said of skittish horses that they had 'taken the boggart'.

There is now a brewery in Manchester called the Boggart Brewery.

WITCHES

The sixteenth century was not a good time to be thought of as having special gifts. In fact, even if you did not have any special gifts you had to beware of being used as a scapegoat. If the milk curdled or cattle died or the river dried up or a baby died, people could always find somebody to blame. The fact that catastrophes and misfortune are just an integral part of nature never occurred to most people; they needed someone to blame and the consequences for the person or persons chosen were frequently severe or even fatal.

In Lancashire a particular group of unfortunates who fell foul of this way of viewing the world have come to be known as the Pendle Witches.

Even today, a traveller to Pendle Hill is likely to be struck by the spooky atmosphere of the place, but in the seventeenth century, when the remote and uninhabited nature of the area gave it a reputation for being godless, the pervasive eeriness would have been of a different magnitude altogether. If we add to this the universally held superstitious beliefs of the time, we have the perfect concoction for the dreadful deeds that took place in 1612.

On 20 August, the so-called Lancashire, or Pendle, Witches were tried and found guilty of witchcraft, murder and other heinous crimes in Lancaster and promptly condemned to death. The cause was what in our more enlightened times would be considered a trifling affair in which the evidence for any kind of malpractice was so flimsy as to be totally non-existent.

A half-blind, simple-minded 80-year-old woman, Mother Demdike, who had lived all her life begging along the lanes and byways of ancient Lancashire, had a granddaughter called Alizon, who was also a beggar. One day, as she was plying her trade near the Lancashire town of Colne, she came across a pedlar and asked him to let her have a few pins (a valuable commodity in those days) but he refused and what happened next is the crux of the story. Alizon put a curse on the pedlar and, believe it or not, a few minutes later the poor man suffered a stroke. He lived just long enough to tell of what had happened to him and of Alizon's curse, before he died. Nowadays this would hardly be seen as cause and effect (pure coincidence would be the more likely explanation) but in the seventeenth century the fatal stroke was seen as a direct result of the curse. The authorities immediately detected the unmistakable whiff of witchcraft and further enquiries were begun. Now all sorts of charges, accusations and insinuations began to crawl out from beneath the woodwork. Alizon confessed to being heavily involved with witchcraft and implicated other local people who did more than just dabble in a little of the occult for personal

The Eye of God

In the tiny hamlet of Newchurch-in-Pendle, nestling in the Lancashire Fells, St Mary's Church has a carving on the tower of what is supposed to be the imitation of the eye of God. The implication is that it is an all-seeing eye with the power to protect churchgoers from the evil doings of witches. It dates from the seventeenth century and could well have been carved about the time of the Pendle Witches.

relaxation. Another crone, Old Chattox, and Mother Demdike were both accused of being witches and murderers, and as the 'witch hunt' progressed more 'evidence' was unearthed. A blemish on the skin of Mother Demdike was declared irrefutable 'proof' that she had been in league with the Devil and that it marked the spot where the Devil had sucked the old woman's blood.

But the most chilling 'evidence' of all was that of another of Demdike's granddaughters. Jennet, a 9-year-old girl, who probably did not have a clue what she was saying, testified against her own mother and swore that she had seen her taking part in activities associated with Devil worship. Her 'evidence' was believed and nine 'witches' were taken to Gallows Hill in Lancaster and hanged. The tenth, one Elizabeth Southerns, cheated the hangman by dying whilst in prison awaiting trial.

SOME SUPERSTITIONS

In Lancashire, as in most places all over the world, there is no shortage of weird and wonderful beliefs and sayings. Most of them belong to a bygone age when ignorant folk sought desperately for explanations of phenomena they could not understand, or to protect themselves from forces against which they had no discernible defences. Here are a few of them:

If a red-haired man or woman is the first person to enter your house on New Year's Day you had better get ready for a bad year.

If you want to have good luck, one way of ensuring it is to grab hold of a black snail by the horns and throw it over your left shoulder.

Another use for snails was in the field of folk medicine. A person suffering from warts was advised to rub them with a black snail. The treatment was only effective if, after the snail had been rubbed on the warts, it was then impaled on a hawthorn.

If the trick with the snails proved less than effective, Lancashire folklore had another way of getting rid of warts. – count up all the warts and then gather the same number of small pebbles and put them into a little bag. The bag then had to be thrown over the left shoulder and the warts would be immediately transferred to the first person to pick it up.

If your left ear feels as if it is burning you can be sure that somebody is speaking well of you or even singing your praises. On the other hand, it your right ear feels as if it is burning you should be on your guard because somebody is saying some pretty nasty things about you.

If a baker wants to make sure that his bread turns out the way it is supposed to, all he has to do is make the sign of a cross on it with his finger. And if a dairyman puts a red-hot poker into the cream during churning, any witches hiding in the churn will be expelled and the cream will not curdle.

Never cut your fingernails or toenails on a Friday or Sunday. If you do, you will inevitably bring bad luck on yourself.

If you want to know how long you will live, here's a tip: cut off a handful of hair and throw it on a fire. If it burns brightly you will have a long life, but if it just disappears in a puff of smoke, don't start reading any long books.

A hagstone (a stone with a naturally occurring hole in it) can be treated much the same as a horseshoe. If you hang it up in a stable it will guard the horses inside and if a man hangs one over his bed he will enjoy the same degree of protection.

THE GHOSTS

There are hundreds, if not thousands, of reports of ghosts in Lancashire. There are haunted houses, haunted pubs, haunted streets and even haunted fairgrounds just about everywhere throughout the county. The tiny villages have them, the market towns have them and so do the sprawling conurbations such as Liverpool and Manchester. So let's have a look at some:

Liverpool: One of the main shopping areas in Liverpool surrounds the once elegant Bold Street, and over the years there have been reports of some very odd goings on there. Several people have reported that as they walked along the pavement they were suddenly transported back to an earlier century and found themselves walking along a cobbled street, surrounded by people wearing Victorian-style clothes.

In the 1980s, in Hale Road, Speke, there were several reports of poltergeist activity. The occupants of the house swore that shadows could mysteriously and suddenly appear on the walls of the living room, books would unaccountably move from one side of the room to another and the toilet would occasionally flush entirely of its own accord.

In Woolton, one of the leafy 'posh' suburbs of Liverpool, there was talk in the 1970s of certain unexplained activities in the old Ambulance Training Centre. The building was reported as the stomping ground of a former policeman whose ghost (affectionately referred to as the 'Sarge') seemed to have taken up residence and was not averse to giving the ambulance men the occasional shiver down their spines. The policeman in question had been driving through Woolton some years earlier when the wheel of his car struck a bollard and he was thrown out and killed instantly as he hit the ground. People who worked in the training centre in the '70s spoke of doors which locked and unlocked themselves, windows which shattered for no apparent reason and footsteps which could be heard in empty rooms.

Another venue for spooky sightings is Lime Street, the main thoroughfare. For at least a couple of hundred years witnesses have claimed that they have seen a tall figure (of indeterminate gender) gliding along Lime Street, its mouth moving as if in conversation. A nearby hotel, possibly the Adelphi, has also supposedly been the spooky abode for a tall, spectral woman. Is it the same woman? Who can tell?

Manchester: Some time in the 1840s a man claimed that, on a visit to Manchester Cathedral, he saw his sister standing in the nave. This was a bit of a surprise to him as he was certain that she was somewhere else a long way from Manchester. Nevertheless, he walked up to her but before he could speak to her she seemed to just evaporate into thin air. The very next day the poor man received news that his sister had died in a tragic accident at precisely the time he 'saw' her in the cathedral.

At a place called Boggart Hole Clough, near Manchester, there was a farm which, according to reports, was once home to what seems to have been a schizophrenic ghost. There were

days when the 'presence' would help the owners with their daily chores, such as washing up, cleaning and sweeping. But at other times it would pull the sheets and blankets off them as they slept and make thumping and banging noises in the middle of the night. Eventually the farmer and his wife had had enough; they told their friendly neighbourhood spook that they were going to sell the farm and move away. Alarmingly, the spook replied, telling them that he would follow wherever they went. In the end the couple decided to stay put and save on the removal expenses.

Blackpool: Every fairground worth its salt has a ghost train, but, according to local legend, Blackpool's has a real ghost. Those who operate the train tell of the frequently heard sound of a man walking through the passageways wearing a pair of clogs. It is generally assumed that the clogs belong to the ghost of a former employee and, not surprisingly, he is referred to as 'Clogger'. Another popular attraction on the same pleasure beach, the Tunnel of Love, is also claimed to be haunted by the spectre of a woman wearing bloodstained clothes.

Not far away, in Blackpool's Victoria Hospital, there were several reports in 2004 of strange goings-on happening on one of the wards. Several members of staff claimed that as they were walking through this particular ward, they felt their clothes being tugged at as though somebody very small (possibly a child) was trying to attract their attention. When they turned round they were astonished to find that there was nobody there. One cleaner who experienced this 'happening' was so startled that she went into hysterics and it took other hospital staff some time to calm her down.

A bit further back, – 1936 to be exact – a taxi driver had to make a stop for some reason in front of the local crematorium. You can imagine his surprise when a green face with dark sunken eyes seemed to appear from nowhere and started staring through the windscreen. We don't know how the taxi driver reacted, but his passenger screamed, jumped out of the taxi and ran off down the road.

Lancaster: Another paranormal experience involving a taxi was reported north of Lancaster in 1974. The driver was going along in his empty taxi when he just happened to look in his rear-view mirror. He was astonished to see a woman sitting in the back of his cab. He pulled over to the side of the road and turned round to speak to the lady, but she had vanished. Thinking his eyes must have been playing tricks on him, he started the engine and moved off down the road again. A few minutes later he glanced in his rear-view mirror and was horrified to see that the woman had reappeared and was sitting just behind him. This time he was too scared to stop and just kept on driving (no doubt with the hairs on the back of his neck standing on end) and eventually the spectre disappeared, never to return.

Southport: In the 1990s a middle-aged couple reported to relatives that something very odd had happened to them in their mobile home on the outskirts of the town. They woke up one night pouring with sweat and could not understand why they were feeling so hot. It was mid-summer but the weather had not been particularly warm and, in any case, they only had a light sheet on the bed and should have been able to sleep comfortably till morning. When the husband got out of bed, he felt the radiator and it was burning hot! He looked at the thermostat and could not believe his eyes: it had been turned to 'MAX', even though the heating had not been used since early Spring. The next night, the thermostat was not touched (it had now been re-set at 'MIN'), but the wife woke up when she felt something heavy on her feet and, when she looked towards the end of the bed, was horrified to see her grandmother (who had been dead for about twenty years) sitting there and covering up her feet with the sheet. The woman then heard her grandmother speak, telling her she must be careful not to get cold!

Chipping: This beautiful little village nestled in the Ribble Valley has a tale to tell which could make all but the stoniest hearts weep. In the 1830s, Lizzie Dean, a pretty scullery maid at the Sun Inn on Windy Street, fell in love with a handsome young man who swore that he was just as much in love with her. She probably put up some token resistance to his amorous advances but the inevitable happened and she found herself 'in the family way'. But if Lizzie was surprised to find herself pregnant, there was an even bigger shock coming her way. Her young lover refused to marry her and, to make matters infinitely worse, he suddenly announced that he was going to marry her best friend. It was too much for the poor girl and she decided on a macabre act of revenge. On the morning of the wedding, in St Bartholomew's Church, which is directly opposite the Sun Inn, she hanged herself, leaving a note stating that she wished to be buried by the entrance to the church so that her ex-lover and wife would have to walk past her grave every time they went to church.

Her wish was granted and her grave can still be seen by visitors today with the simple epitaph 'Elizabeth Dean 5th November 1835', but in an unconsecrated part of the church grounds.

Today, there are more than just a few residents of, and visitors to, Chipping's Sun Inn who claim that they have seen a girl fitting Lizzie's description haunting various rooms in the pub.

THE STATELY HOMES

Just about every stately home in Britain boasts at least one resident ghost and those in Lancashire are no exception. Here are a few:

Chingle Hall: To be found just outside Preston, Chingle Hall is a thirteenth-century moated manor house which has claimed a resident ghost since the late 1600s. According to legend, the building underwent some major renovation work in the seventeenth century and while the work was being completed considerable additions were made to the original construction, including several priest holes.

Chingle Hall was the birthplace of a certain John Wall who grew up to be a Catholic priest at a time in England's history when Catholicism amounted to heresy and was punishable by death. Indeed, Father John Wall, as he became known, was executed for his faith in 1679. For some reason his head was sent off to France but, after some time, it was returned to Lancashire where it was buried somewhere in the grounds behind Chingle Hall. His spirit is now said to glide about the building, floating in and out of all the rooms, giving visitors the occasional fright. Local legend adds that if and when the head is discovered the ghost of John Wall will find peace and will no longer feel the need to haunt the property.

Heskin Hall: Near Chorley, this is now a conference centre and wedding venue, but if the tales are true, its walls guard a very grizzly history. The original building was erected in the sixteenth century and by common consent is recognised as one of the finest examples of Tudor architecture that Lancashire has to offer.

The spooky story associated with this house dates back to the seventeenth century and concerns a simple peasant girl who had been brought up in the Catholic faith and who had total trust in her local priest. But it was this trust which would eventually claim her life when her priest betrayed her in a cowardly and shameful way. Cromwell's Roundheads arrived one day looking for the Catholic priest who they thought was hiding in or near Heskin Hall. When they found him he swore that he had renounced Catholicism and offered to prove it by not only denouncing the poor peasant girl of that religion but by also hanging her himself. The officer in charge agreed that the execution should go ahead and so the woman was hanged by the priest from a beam in the house. However, it appears that the priest's protestations and shameful demonstration of his apostasy did him little good; Cromwell's soldiers did not really believe him so they hanged him as well.

The White Lady, as she is now known, haunts the whole building, although she does seem to have a preference for what is generally referred to as the Scarlet Room.

Rufford Old Hall: Near Ormskirk, this is the haunting ground of another unfortunate lady, but one of a slightly different colour – the Grey Lady. Rufford Old Hall dates back to about 1530 and was originally built by Sir Thomas Hesketh, whose family owned it until 1936 when it was handed over to The National Trust.

The Grey Lady is supposed to be the unquiet spirit of Elizabeth Hesketh who lived in the hall at the time of the English Civil War. If the story is to be believed she married a military man, whom she loved deeply, but he was called away to fight before the wedding feast was even over. She waited and waited for his return but had to endure a long period when there was absolutely no news of her husband. Then, out of the blue, a soldier appeared who had served with Elizabeth's absent husband and assured her that he was unharmed and was making his way back to his bride. A great welcoming feast was prepared but there was no sign of him. Nor did he appear the next day, or the next week and, as the weeks became months and the months became years, Elizabeth pined and waited, but it was in vain. She died without ever seeing her beloved husband again. Before her death she swore that she would never leave Rufford Old Hall until her husband returned, and her spirit is still there, waiting, hoping …

Samlesbury Hall: Situated between Blackburn and Preston lies another manor house which claims to be home to the wandering souls of long-departed residents. The house was built in 1325 originally as the home for a certain Gilbert de Southworth and his family. It has, however, been through several reincarnations and has, in its time, also been a public house and a boarding school for girls.

It is reputed to be haunted by, among others, the ghost of Lady Dorothy Southworth. She was madly in love with a handsome young scion of the Hoghton family and they hoped to be joined in holy matrimony and spend the rest of their lives together in wedded bliss. But there was just one problem: religion. The Southworths were staunchly Catholic and the Hoghtons were Protestant, and so what followed was a Romeo and Juliet style family feud, with neither family wanting their offspring

to marry into the other. The young lovers planned to elope but their intentions were discovered and Dorothy's brother killed her lover in front of her. She was horror stricken and, so they say, went mad with grief before she eventually died still pining for her intended. It is supposed to be her spirit that can be seen floating in and out of the rooms and along the corridors, still sobbing for her murdered sweetheart.

5

FOLK CUSTOMS

Many of the folk customs of Lancashire, like those in other parts of the country, have their origins in ancient religious beliefs, Christianity, mysterious superstitions or are nothing more than an excuse for a bit of a party to relieve the monotony of the daily grind. Many Lancashire customs are now just memories or subjects for folklorists to write about. However, some have survived and still provide communal entertainment of a traditional kind.

PACE EGGING

At one time Pace Egging was a custom practiced all over Lancashire. Traditionally linked to Easter time, it is still observed in one form or another in different parts of the county, although it is perhaps not as popular a sport as it once was.

The origins of this kind of annual entertainment provide a perfect example of how Christianity and pre-Christian pagan customs have fused together. The egg has been a universal symbol of fertility and the renewal of life since the dawn of time, and its symbolic use around Easter time has far more to do with primitive religions than with Christianity. On the other hand the word 'pace' is derived from the Anglo-Saxon for Easter, *pasche* which in turn has its counterparts in other European languages (French has *Pâques,* Spanish has *Pascua*) so the term 'pace egging' is really just another way of saying

'Easter Egging'. Ultimately, the term is derived from the Hebrew term *Pesakh*, which we know as Passover.

Pace Egging still survives in places such as Preston where every Easter Monday people gather in Avenham Park to roll their highly decorated hard-boiled eggs down a grassy bank to see if they will reach the bottom without cracking.

Nowadays, these activities are just about the whole celebration but in former times the day was taken up with lively entertainment. Traditionally, people would get up in the morning and have boiled eggs for breakfast. Then the egg shells were either used for improvised games or given to the 'Pace Eggers'. These were locals who donned exotic, outlandish costumes (animal skins, funny hats etc.) and painted their faces before setting off, dancing and prancing through the Lancashire villages. As they went along they sang traditional songs and asked for money or eggs as a reward. Usually the procession included certain stock characters, such as the Noble Youth, the Lady Gay, the Soldier Brave and the drunken layabout known as Old Tosspot.

In recent years attempts have been made to bring this ancient bit of seasonal fun back to life in all its former glory, particularly in and around Rochdale where schoolchildren have been encouraged to take part in its revival.

The village of Holcombe, near Ramsbottom, is the venue for a very similar sport, but this egg-rolling festival takes place on Good Friday. The traditional celebrations in Holcombe, however, still retain something of a Christian element. The day begins with a church service at the bottom of Holcombe Hill, a hill which many see as a replica of the hill at Calvary, the site of the crucifixion. (Fortunately, there is no attempt to repeat the events of the original Good Friday!) These days the activities are aimed at creating an atmosphere of fun and relaxation and so, after the church service, everyone makes their way up to the top of the hill and at about midday they begin rolling their eggs to the bottom. The children then eat the eggs (these days most of them are made of chocolate) while a good number of the adults avail themselves of the hospitality on offer at the two public houses conveniently situated at the bottom of the hill.

THE BURNING OF JUDAS

One of the more gruesome celebrations that used to take place in Liverpool, until it was banned by the authorities in the 1960s, was the Burning of Judas. This was a custom not dissimilar to the universal practice of burning an effigy of Guy Fawkes on Bonfire Night, but it was confined to a largely Catholic area around the southern suburb of the Dingle. The whole point of the celebration was to burn a Judas Iscariot in effigy every Good Friday, as a symbolic punishment for his betrayal of Christ.

This custom is still alive in other parts of the world, particularly in South America and Catholic European countries, and there are those who say that it was brought to Liverpool by sailors from places such a Mexico, Spain and Portugal. What has not been explained, however, is why the bonfires only burned in a very small enclave near Liverpool docks. There are many other parts of Liverpool with substantial Catholic communities but the practice never spread to them.

GRAVY WRESTLING

In Stacksteads, a village near Bacup, there is an annual event which has to rank among the wackiest in the country's sporting calendar: the Gravy Wrestling competition. Competitors have to wrestle in a paddling pool containing 100 litres of gravy for at least two minutes and are awarded points for technique and crowd appeal. Unsurprisingly, the prize every contestant wins is a good hose-down after the contest.

SADDLEWORTH RUSHCART RACING

Saddleworth is one of those places which pose problems for anyone attempting to write about the geography of England. Its situation has meant that, as politicians have seen fit to meddle with the historical county borders, it has tended to move back and forth between two northern counties. It was once considered part of Yorkshire even though, theologically speaking, it was always in the Diocese of Rochdale (Lancashire) and is now officially part of Oldham (Greater Manchester, formally Lancashire). Therefore its rushcart racing can legitimately be mentioned here.

Centuries ago, churches in Lancashire did not have proper flooring, they just had an earthen surface. In order to make things a little more comfortable and probably keep parishioners' feet warm during the service, straw or grass would be strewn on the ground. The best time of year to do this was the summer, when there was plenty of mown grass available and it could be dried out thoroughly before being brought indoors. It had to be conveyed from the fields and this was best done by cart. When the sturdy village lads were driving the carts to the church an element of competition inevitably became part of the task and lo and behold, a race was born!

Nowadays, all the churches in the area have proper flooring, along with other mod cons, but the idea of the race has survived, and so every August hay carts are piled high with grass or straw (to a height of 15ft) on top of which a driver sits. These days one of the local Morris dancers also sits atop the hay and 'encourages' the hundred or so other Morrismen who are pulling the carts for all they are worth through the surrounding villages. The whole event is treated as a day out for the communities with stalls selling cakes and pies, clubs putting on displays, gurning competitions (designed to see who can pull the ugliest face) and (surprise, surprise!) a few drinks in the nearby pubs.

MORRIS DANCING

Morris dancing has long been popular in most parts of Britain (and many places abroad) and Lancashire is no exception. Many events throughout the county echo to the sound of wooden sticks clacking and bells jingling as the performers entertain the appreciative crowds. But if we start to enquire into the origins of this form of entertainment there are some surprises in store for us.

The first question is why 'Morris' dancing, and where did the term come from? It is now universally accepted that 'Morris' is a corruption (or perhaps just an earlier spelling) of the word Moorish. So what are 'Moorish' dancers doing in Lancashire? For the answer we have to travel back in time and space to fifteenth-century Spain. In 1492, the King and Queen of Castille, Ferdinand and Isabella, drove the Arabs (or Moors) out of Spain and back into North Africa. These Arab peoples had ruled almost the whole of Spain for 700 years and when they were finally driven out of the country it was a cause for great celebrations. Part of the celebrations involved the invention of a new form of dancing which, in Spanish, became known as *moresca* dancing. This is the word that eventually evolved into our 'Morris', and it is thought that the word entered the English language after Henry VII invited exponents of the art to perform at his Christmas celebrations.

There are several different styles of Morris dancing in England and Wales, but the variety performed in Lancashire is distinguished from the others by several features. Aficionados claim that the Lancashire version is more military in style, tempo and content. Perhaps this is because most of the performers were employed in the mills and a more vigorous style of dancing allowed them to let off steam and provided a more strenuous form of exercise. Another feature which distinguishes the Lancashire style from the other versions is the involvement of women. Until recently, the Cotswolds, the Borders and Northumberland Morris dancing styles did not include women and the activity was generally perceived as an all-male preserve. But, at least from the eighteenth century, Lancashire-style Morris dancing has always included roles for women.

In Bacup there is a rather special type of dancing performed by the Coco-nut Dancers, which may or may not be derived from the more widely known Morris dancing. Some claim that the dances were brought to England by Moorish pirates but others are convinced that the first 'Nutters' came up from Cornwall to work in the Lancashire mines and brought their unique form of entertainment with them.

Whatever their origins, their big day is always Easter Saturday when they assemble at nine o'clock in the morning at the Travellers' Rest public house and, perform their merry dances from one side of the town to the other, to the accompaniment of a local silver band. The usual description for their activities is that they dance 'from boundary to boundary'.

If the Nutters' form of entertainment is related to Morris dancing it is hard to tell from their clothes. They wear a distinctive costume, which is basically a kind of white skirt with horizontal red bands and, attached to their knees, hands and belts, are wooden disks (the 'coconuts') which are banged together in time to the music. The Nutters also blacken their faces and there are at least two explanations for this tradition: many of the dancers were originally from the mines and so the association here is with coal dust; the other reason suggested is that it made it more difficult for individual dancers to be recognised by evil spirits if they offended them in any way during their performance.

CLOG COBBIN

If you are ever at a loose end on an Easter Monday and don't fancy egg rolling or going to church, you might fancy watching or indulging in the wacky Lancashire sport of 'clog cobbin'. This is the gentle art of picking up a clog (only proper ones with wooden soles and leather uppers are allowed) and throwing it as far as you can. However, there is just one catch: the competition takes place on a river bank and you have to throw the clog backwards over your shoulder. And if the clog lands in the river you are immediately disqualified.

Clog cobbin cannot claim to be a noble and ancient tradition with its origins lost in the mists of time. In fact, it only came about in the 1970s when somebody decided it would be a good idea to get grown men to see who could throw their clogs furthest. And of course there are prizes ... usually of the liquid variety and distributed in the Roebuck Inn on Burnley Road. Isn't that a surprise?

THE WORLD BLACK PUDDING THROWING CHAMPIONSHIPS

In a county that prides itself so much on the excellence of its black pudding it was only a matter of time before some clever clogs decided that instead of eating one he would chuck it. Then someone else would try to throw it further and 'before you could say Jack Robinson' another Lancashire sport was born.

The game, as it is played now, has acquired a certain amount of sophistication and involves the Lancastrian's mortal enemy: the Yorkshireman. Nowadays before the contest begins, piles of Yorkshire puddings are placed on top of a 20ft-high plinth. The aim of the game is to throw black puddings up in the air in an attempt to knock one or all of the Yorkshire puddings off the plinth. And the rules of the game are pretty strict: contestants must throw underarm and stand on a special spot known as 'the oche'.

This competition was devised as recently as the 1980s but it harnesses the long-standing mutual antagonism Yorkshiremen and Lancastrians have felt towards each other since the days of the Wars of the Roses in the fifteenth century.

The competition takes place annually on the second Sunday in September, in Ramsbottom.

WAKES WEEKS

When the mill towns of Lancashire were thriving communities and the hundreds of cotton mills worked relentlessly to keep up with production, the thunderous noise of the machinery would deafen anyone in the vicinity for most of the year. But then, as regular as clockwork, for one week in August silence descended on the area and the only people making any kind of noise were the maintenance men giving the looms their annual service. The workers had gone. For one glorious week they did not have to get up in the morning when the 'knocker-up' tapped on their bedroom windows, nor did they have to trudge the cobbled streets to the mills and then back homewards at night, exhausted after a gruelling day, only to have a meagre repast, go to bed and get some sleep before it all started again the next morning.

Until 1907, holidays for the mill workers had been something of a haphazard affair but then, in Lancashire at least, the mill owners agreed to let the workers have a regular 'wakes' holiday by right. It was, however, unpaid. This meant that families had to try to save a little out of their pitiful wages so they could survive during the holiday period. Those who could scrimp and scrape a little more than the others throughout the years would go away for a day or two to places such as Blackpool or Southport to enjoy the bracing sea air, tuck into to fish and chips and buy a couple of 'kiss-me-quick' hats and a stick of rock.

What tends to be forgotten, however, is that 'wakes' holidays have their origins in religion. The word 'wake' is connected with 'awake' but was used in a religious context to mean 'vigil', and denoted that people should 'keep vigil' (i.e. stay awake) all night to attain the correct frame of mind for the religious services to come. The religious association of the wake has long since been forgotten (and the Wakes Weeks themselves have now more or less been absorbed into the normal annual summer holiday enjoyed by all) but the concept and the word itself survive in Irish communities where funerals are still preceded by a vigil or wake.

PRESTON GUILD

In Lancashire if you say that something happens 'every Preston Guild' it is the equivalent of saying that the event takes place 'once in a blue moon' or, in other words, not very often. The roots of this expression relate to the Preston Guild celebrations which only take place every twenty years. The last one was in 2012 and so if you missed it you will now have to wait till 2032 before you get another chance to watch all the fun.

But the regular twenty-year cycle has not always been observed. In fact, in the early days, there does not appear to have been any system applied to the Guild celebrations and before 1562 their occurrence was totally random. We know from the records that Preston Guilds were held in 1329, 1397, 1415, 1459, 1501, 1543 and 1562, at which point it was decided that every twenty years should be the norm. This has been the custom ever since, apart from 1942 when, it had to be cancelled because of the war. Then it was decided to revive the event ten years later, in 1952, and the twenty-year cycle has been observed ever since.

The origins of the Guild date from the very earliest days of the city's history. In 1179, King Henry II granted Preston its first Royal Charter which, in those days, was a momentous event. It gave the burghers of Preston the right to hold markets and fairs and, at the same time, to operate an early form of monopoly capitalism. The Guilds Merchants were legally entitled to control the commercial dealings of the town and, of course, they made sure that they arranged things in such a way that Preston (and the Guild Merchants in particular) were the main beneficiaries of any business arrangements that were agreed upon within the town boundaries. In short, the merchants operated a form of 'closed shop' policy and any outsider who wanted to make a living by trading in Preston had to have special permission. The penalties for not observing the rules could be punitive.

HENRY. II.

The format for the celebrations has changed very little over the centuries, but today there is probably less emphasis on catching illegal traders. It starts off with a ceremony which dates back to the Middle Ages – the opening of the Guild Court when the mayor stands up in his gleaming regalia of office and delivers the opening speech. This is probably the most formal event of the holiday and is timed very precisely. It has to take place on the first Monday after 29 August, the date on which the Beheading of St John the Baptist is remembered.

When the formalities are over and done with a party atmosphere descends over the activities of the rest of the fortnight. There are street processions, street parties, a concert

HENRY II

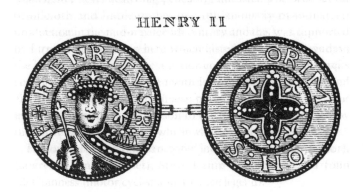

in Avenham Park and then, for those whose taste in music is a little more high-brow, a Proms in the Park concert. All in all it is a pretty impressive achievement of historical continuity, and Preston can take pride in the fact that it is unique. Nowhere else in Britain can boast medieval Guild celebrations that have lasted so long.

CLOG DANCING

There are two types of clog: one is the hardy, tough clog designed for rough wear down the mines and in the mills and factories; the other type are known as 'neet' clogs, which are not as robust and may or may not have patterned or decorated leather uppers, which are clogs for dancing.

There is clog dancing of one sort or another in many parts of the world, but equally Lancashire's variety also enjoys worldwide renown. Those who are skilled in the art will tell you that the Lancashire style came about in the 1800s or 1900s when clog-wearing mill workers started tapping their feet in time with the noise made by the looms. Eventually, a habit seemingly developed out of the repetitious, monotonous clatter of the machines evolved into a fascinating form of popular entertainment.

The very first 'cloggers' would have displayed their skill and artistry as they were performing more mundane tasks, such as looking after the looms or supervising other workers as they slaved away in deafening surroundings among potentially dangerous machines. If they were any good they also tended to do a bit of moonlighting, dancing on street corners and perhaps earning a few coppers for their efforts. The very best exponents would have made it into the Music Halls, one of the few forms of entertainment open to the working man in the nineteenth century. The opportunity to 'turn pro' was a prize worth striving for; it could take a talented dancer out of the daily grind of life in the mills or down the pits and more or less guarantee him a standard of living which otherwise would have remained beyond his reach.

But the mill workers and miners who became such devotees of the cloggers' art were not the only kids on the block. Whereas the rhythm of the spinning looms set the tone of their particular brand of dancing, the folk who plied the waters of northern canals also developed their own style of clog dancing. These people took their cue from the 'chug-chug' rhythm of the steam engines which propelled the wide boats at a slow but steady pace up and down the northern waterways. Their audience was mainly the habitués of the pubs dotted at irregular intervals along the canal banks. It appears that many of these riparian performers had a special trick which could earn them a few extra coppers. When they had demonstrated their amazing dexterity

Did you know that …

Charlie Chaplin, who was not a Lancastrian, began his life in showbiz as a professional clogger and joined a troupe of clog dancers who called themselves the 'Seven Lancashire Lads'?

Another entertainer who achieved fame in the early world of the cinema was Stan Laurel (Laurel and Hardy) and he started off as a professional clog-dancer? However, as he was born in Ulverston when it was still part of Lancashire, he can claim to be a true Lancastrian.

Most music hall entertainers, whether they were professional cloggers or not, could claim to possess at least rudimentary 'clogging' skills? They usually found that ending their turn with a bit of a clog dance was a good idea, particularly if the audience had not been impressed with the rest of their act.

Ernie Wise (the other half of the Morecambe and Wise duo) also had clog dancing in his act during the 1930s?

on the floor, their *pièce de résistance* was to stand on a table, on which several glasses of ale had been strategically placed, and repeat the display without knocking any of the glasses over or spilling any ale, or, at least, attempt to.

All this sounds very entertaining but, unfortunately, there was another side to Lancastrians' dextrous footwork. As an offshoot of clog dancing there was also a pretty brutal martial art known as 'up and down fighting'. This involved an illegal (but nonetheless practiced) form of settling arguments by, basically, trying to kick the hell out of an opponent while wearing the heavy working-style clogs. Such fights do not seem to have been governed by anything resembling the Marquess of Queensbury rules of boxing. Broken arms and legs were considered nothing more than unfortunate occupational hazards and if a man went down he could be kicked in the head by an adversary wearing size nines; not a good way to end an evening.

THE WHIT WALKS

Whitsuntide, also known as Pentecost, is an ancient Church holiday which was observed in the Middle Ages, not only for its religious significance but also as a kind of mini-break for agricultural labourers before the arrival of summer and the need to prepare for the hard work of gathering in the harvest. The term Pentecost was brought in by the Normans. Until their arrival the date had always been referred to in Anglo-Saxon as 'whitsun'; this in turn was derived from the original 'White Sunday', so called because babies being baptised at that time were obliged to be wrapped in white christening robes. Presumably, at other times of the year the proud parents could wrap their infants in whatever coloured cloths they happened to possess.

In Lancashire, as elsewhere, Whitsun is traditionally observed with interdenominational church gatherings characterised by a walk through towns and villages and culminating in what the

church authorities considered to be a socially acceptable form of communal entertainment. The more licentious behaviour which characterised the Spring rites of secular organisations was frowned upon.

The origin of the Whit Walks, as we know them today, can be dated to 19 July 1821, when all the Sunday school children of Manchester walked in procession to mark the coronation of King George IV. Whether or not this was originally intended to be a one-off event we cannot be sure. All we know is that it became an annual celebration and was seized upon by the mill owners and workers alike who felt the need for some sort of a late Spring holiday.

In Lancashire the Whit Walks have another significance. Either by accident or design, the walks always coincide with Brass Band competitions, particularly in Saddleworth and what is now Thameside. This, along with the sausage rolls, black puddings and fizzy drinks on sale, adds to the holiday atmosphere.

6

LANCASTRIAN INVENTIONS

If you ever go and watch a football match, spend hours browsing the internet on a computer, put a mac on when it's raining, or suck on a 'Fisherman's Friend' while you wait to have your car unclamped, you might be surprised to know how much the history of Lancashire is involved with all of these activities ... and many more besides. Native or adopted Lancastrians have played a huge but largely unsung role in the lives of nearly all of us. And any Scotsmen reading this should brace themselves; there are those who claim that the kilt and the haggis are Lancashire inventions!

Goal nets: Shropshire-born John Alexander Brodie (1858–1934) began his career as a civil engineer with the Mersey Docks and Harbour Board in Liverpool. However, as a gifted and ambitious professional he soon moved on to greater things, both at home and abroad. He served as President of the Institution of Civil Engineers and was appointed Associate Professor of Engineering at Liverpool University. He was also a founder member of the organisation we now know as The Royal Automobile Club. In addition to all of this he was one of the first people to come up with the idea of solving the housing shortage by pre-fabrication, an invention which was to prove a godsend in Liverpool after the Second World War.

Most people would probably think that his greatest achievement was the construction of the first Mersey Tunnel (completed in 1934), but not John Alexander Brodie. He was the man who, in 1889, designed and invented goalpost netting, which is such a crucial feature of any football pitch, and this was the invention of which he always claimed to be most proud.

The 'Mac': Charles Macintosh was born in Glasgow in 1766 (he died, also in Glasgow, in 1843) and has kept more people dry in inclement weather than he could ever have imagined. He grew up in his native city where his father owned a chemical works and so it is hardly surprising that as a 'wee boy' Charles became fascinated with the mysterious wonders of the science of chemistry. As he got older his interest in chemicals stayed with him and inevitably drew him towards a life of scientific enquiry and discovery. Then one day he had the bright idea of trying to find a method of making cloth waterproof and devising a way of keeping people dry when the heavens opened. Until then, coats and clothing had simply soaked up the rain until they were a soggy heavy mass. Charles was looking for a way of manufacturing clothes which would shed most, if not all, of the rainwater.

Other people had tried to do this but it was Charles who eventually came up with a solution which was both scientifically sound and commercially feasible. In 1823 he took out a patent on an invention which revolutionised the textile industry. He worked out how to bind a layer of rubber in-between two layers of cloth, and waterproof cloth was born. A year later, in 1824, Charles struck up a partnership with Hugh Birley, a Manchester businessman with an interest in textiles. They opened a factory and in no time at all had produced the world's first commercially viable waterproof coat (with the brand name 'Mackintosh'; note the included 'k') and, to use a well-worn cliché, the rest is history. Within a year the factory was turning out waterproof 'macs' by the thousand and the business partnership just went from strength to strength.

The kilt: There is probably no more enduring icon associated with Scotland than the kilt. It has symbolised the land north of the border for centuries, adorned biscuit tins and whisky bottles for as long as anyone can remember, and it has been the fount of all those jokes about what a Scotsman wears underneath it. Yet there is a body of opinion which says that the kilt as we know it today was the invention of (heaven forefend!) an Englishman.

We know from historical records that the original Celts in Scotland wore trousers but, certainly in the highlands, trousers can be very uncomfortable. They get wet with all the tramping through the heather and, on cold nights, they provide no protection at all. So, probably around the fifteenth or sixteenth century, the highlanders invented the 'big kilt', which was one long length of material wrapped around the waist and thrown over the right or left shoulder. This had two main advantages over trousers: it did not get wet as the wearer walked through long grass or heather and, at night, it could double up as a blanket (the Gaelic word for this garment, *plaid,* meant 'blanket').

Then, sometime in the 1720s, a certain Quaker gentleman from Lancashire, Thomas Rawlinson, entered the scene. He was working in Scotland and took to wearing highland dress but he found it unwieldy and cumbersome, so he came up with the idea of chopping it up a bit and rearranging pieces here and there. One of his bright ideas was to separate the bit that went around the waist from the bit that went over the shoulder; obviously the length of cloth  around the waist became the kilt as we know it today.

If this were not bad news enough for the Scots, there is more to come. It is also claimed that the savoury delight haggis, made famous by Scotland's national poet Robert Burns (which he named 'the chieftain o' the puddin' race') is not Scottish either. In fact, those persons who come out with this outrageous claim believe, once again, that this wonderful accompaniment to a tot or two of whisky, was invented in ... Lancashire! Those who are rash enough to make this claim base their argument on the book *Liber Cure Cocorum* ('The Art of Cooking'), which was produced in Lancashire in 1430. The book contains the following 'haggis' recipe:

> Take the heart of a sheep, its kidneys and the rest of the insides, mix them up thoroughly and then boil well. Then hack it all together and mix in herbs according to season ... hyssop, sage, parlsley and season to taste.

The Lancastrian author does not mention the whisky though.

Graphene: This is the new buzzword in the scientific community. It is claimed to be the wonderful new material which will revolutionise just about every human activity when its full potential is realised over the coming decades. But just what is it that makes graphene so fantastic? The answer is that it combines physical properties which are not found in any other single material: it is simultaneously as hard as diamond, as flexible as rubber and conducts electricity at least as well as copper. Proponents see applications in the world of medicine, technology and industry where long-standing problems will be solved almost overnight. It is also highly likely that within a very short time the world will benefit from e-paper, which will allow us to develop television and computer screens which can be rolled up after use like a piece of paper. Massive amounts of money has been invested in graphene all around the world and in Manchester there are plans to build a Graphene Institute at a cost of £61 million.

This unbelievable material is the result of ground-breaking work done by two Russian physicists at the University of Manchester, Sir Andre Geim and Sir Konstantin Novoselov. Both were awarded the Nobel Prize for Physics in 2010 and knighted in 2012.

Computers: We all use them, our lives are governed by them, we can communicate with people all over the world with them, and if they suddenly disappeared from the face of the earth, life as we know it would be impossible. The institution we have to thank for these marvellous machines is, once again, Manchester University, and a certain Alan Turing who worked there from 1949 to 1954.

Alan Turing OBE, FRS was born in London in 1912. His father was in the Indian Civil Service and worked for most of his adult life on the sub-continent, but Alan was brought up and educated in England. At school he was a studious boy who showed an early interest in, and aptitude for, mathematics. From his early teens his academic career was already mapped out for him: he studied at Cambridge, taught at Cambridge and then spent some time in America before returning to England in 1938. By now the dark clouds of war were on the horizon and Alan Turing's unique gifts were recognised by certain organisations who were making plans, in case the worst should happen. When the worst did happen, Alan Turing found himself working in Bletchley Park, the HQ of the government's Code and Cipher School. Here his genius proved vital to the war work carried on at the school, and he and his team developed a machine capable of cracking the German Enigma encryption machine.

When the war was finally over Alan's talents had to find a new outlet and in 1949 he took up a post at Manchester University, where he worked in the field of artificial intelligence. His work, both at Bletchley and Manchester, laid the foundations for information technology as we know it today.

Fisherman's Friend: Back in 1865 a Fleetwood chemist by the name of James Lofthouse thought he would try to find the solution to an age-old problem: what could be done to help people who suffered from chronic coughs and chest complaints during the winter? His particular concern was with the breathing problems which seemed to plague the brave men who took their tiny boats up to the Icelandic fishing grounds in order to put fish on the tables of British homes.

His answer to the problem came first of all as a liquid, then in lozenge form, made of menthol, eucalyptus and other natural ingredients which combined to produce a natural cough medicine and expectorant. Fisherman's Friends are still going strong and still produced in Fleetwood, Lancashire.

Sugar cubes: A young lad from Chorley is credited with making sugar easier to handle and putting those delicate little cubes into dishes on the tables of tea-shops, cafés and restaurants.

Henry Tate (later Sir Henry Tate) was the son of a Chorley clergyman who decided at a very early age that he was not going to follow in his father's footsteps. At the age of 13 he began an apprenticeship in the grocery business and by the age of 20 had already opened his own shop. Pretty soon business was booming and he opened another shop, and then another until, at the age of 35, he owned five grocery shops which were bringing him a very healthy income. In fact, over his lifetime he earned so much money that he was able to found Liverpool University Library in 1892 and create the Tate Art Gallery in London in 1897.

In 1872 he either patented or acquired the patent (there is some discussion about this) to produce sugar in the manageable little cubes which we know today. Until then it would arrive at the grocers' shops in huge, heavy blocks before it had to be literally sawn into smaller hunks to be sold to customers.

Lancashire's 'Denver Boot': If you take a chance and park your car where parking is forbidden and return to find it immobilized by a great metal contraption that bears a slight resemblance to some medieval implement of torture, remember that you have a Prestonian to thank for your predicament. As the name implies, the original wheel clamp was first designed and produced in Denver, Colorado USA, but various designs on the theme have appeared in different parts of the world. The design adopted in Britain is officially termed the 'London Wheel Clamp' and was the brainchild of a certain Trevor Whitehouse, a native of Preston ... *thanks a lot, Trev*!

The Flying Shuttle: Traditional weaving in Lancashire, as everywhere else, was a slow and laborious task. Handloom operators had to spend hours at the loom throwing a very basic shuttle containing the weft back and forth from one side of the loom to the other between the warps. If the cloth being produced was broadloom two people were needed – one to throw the shuttle and one to catch it and throw it back. But then John Kay came along. Born in Walmersby, just outside Bury, in 1704, his father was a yeoman farmer. John was apprenticed to a weaver but mastered the art so quickly that he soon got bored with the mind-numbing tedium of hours and days spent passing the shuttle from hand-to-hand through the weft and warp. So he developed a contraption which would throw a modified shuttle automatically from one side of the loom to the other, carrying the warp through the weft as it went. This was to produce two great improvements on the old system; not only was the whole process speeded up considerably, but the need for the second operator was done away with. Unfortunately, few of the weavers who earned their crust at the traditional looms shared his enthusiasm for the time and labour-saving invention. In fact, they feared for their livelihoods and John Kay's home was attacked. He received little, if any, financial reward for his efforts and fled to France where he died in poverty in 1778.

The Spinning Jenny: Born about 1720 into a humble family who lived in the Blackburn area, James Hargreaves grew up to be a carpenter and weaver. He had no formal education but did have an inquisitive mind and an abiding fascination for all things mechanical. At that time in Lancashire many families supplemented their day job incomes by spinning and weaving on primitive contraptions which they kept at home. Hargreaves was well acquainted with these machines from an early age and then, one day, suddenly realised that he could probably improve on their design and efficiency. After some thought and tinkering about with drawings, plans and ideas, in 1764, he produced a machine which any historian of the times will know as a 'spinning jenny'. It was a considerable improvement on what had gone before and was a great labour-saving device; the operator could spin eight threads single-handedly. But although it was no doubt an advancement in textile technology, it did have its drawbacks as the thread it produced snapped easily and tended to be rather coarse. Another drawback was that, like with

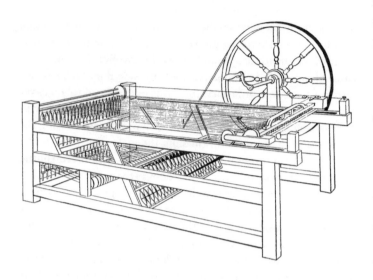

the Flying Shuttle, many workers regarded the spinning jenny as a threat to their livelihoods. A mob of Lancashire spinners decided to take matters into their own hands and marched on Hargreaves's factory and destroyed the machine which he had so painstakingly built. However, the hammers that smashed the first spinning jenny could not prevent the course of history. Hargreaves failed to apply to take out a patent on his invention until 1770, by which time many others had recognised that the future lay in such modernising equipment and so, within a short space of time, dozens of similar devices had been patented. Hargreaves never received the financial rewards to which he should have been entitled. He died in 1778.

Why is Hargreaves's invention referred to as a 'Jenny'?

There are those who maintain that this type of spinning machine was not in fact invented by him, but by Thomas Highs of Leigh who named it after his daughter, Jane.

The Water Frame: A further contribution to the Industrial Revolution was made by another Lancashire lad, Richard Arkwright, who was born in Preston in 1732. He too was born into a poor family (his parents had no fewer than thirteen children to support!) and life must have been tough. He was apprenticed to a barber but then went on to set up his own wig-making business. This meant that he now had to travel around Lancashire collecting, no doubt for a fee, cuttings of human hair. During his travels he heard about attempts being made to devise a machine which would make spinning and weaving a less time-consuming process and thought he would have a go at inventing such a machine himself. What he eventually arrived at was what has come to be known as 'Arkwright's Water Frame'. It was basically an improved spinning jenny but, as the name suggests, it was operated by means of running water and a water wheel. Unlike James Hargreaves, Richard Arkwright became a very rich man after his invention proved to be such a fillip to the Lancashire textile industry. When he died in 1792 it was reported that he was worth over £500,000, an absolutely astronomical sum in those days.

The Spinning Mule: In Bolton, just before Christmas 1753, a lady by the name of Mrs Crompton gave birth to a son who was later christened Samuel. Once again, this family was extremely poor. Samuel's parents were employed in farming, but to eke out their meagre income they spent their evenings carding, spinning and weaving textiles, which they then sold on the Bolton market. As the boy grew up he became more and more involved with his parents' moonlighting activities (he also earned a bit more cash by playing the fiddle in local hostelries), spending much of his time sitting at a Hargreaves's spinning jenny. But his attempts to get to grips with the temperamental machine often proved a source of frustration and annoyance: the thread kept snapping and causing interruptions to his work output. So the young Samuel set about finding a way of improving the Jenny and, after years of trial and error, devised his very own machine. As things turned out, his 'mule' as he called it, was more or less a combination of the good bits of both Arkwright's Water Frame and Hargreaves's spinning jenny. Unfortunately, Crompton was to join the long list of people who came up with brilliant ideas and inventions but profited little from them. His financial rewards from the Spinning Mule were minimal, although his brainchild played an enormously important role in Bolton's later period of successful industrial development. He died in 1827.

The Ossy Splint: Brian Foote (1943–2009) of Oswaldtwistle was a remarkable man. He had few educational qualifications but an inquisitive mind and a passion for solving problems by mechanical means. His inventiveness was to prove a boon not only to himself but to accident victims all over the world. One day in the 1970s Brian suffered a dreadful injury when his right arm came into contact with an angle grinder. He severed the ulna nerve and a tendon, and his recovery involved a prolonged and uncomfortable period of treatment and convalescence. The standard treatment at the time was to put a rigid splint on the injured limb. This type of splint was not only uncomfortable but did little to prevent the problem of 'clawing', and consequently two of Brian's fingers looked as if they were going to be permanently bent. Brian started investigating ways to make his predicament more bearable and within no time at all he had solved the problem. After experimenting he came up with a splint which was basically a kind of glove attached to small springs and levers which protected the injured hand but at the same time allowed a much greater degree of flexibility. This allowed the patient to use his injured hand for a greater range of tasks than was possible before Brian's invention. Orthopaedic departments of hospitals all around the world now use the Ossy Levered Outrigger Splint, although it is more colloquially called 'the Ossy'.

Shorthand: Long before Mr Pitman, Mr Gregg and James Hill (who invented the 'teeline' system) came on the scene, a gentleman from Lancashire devised a system of taking down notes quickly in a way which could only be read by those who had studied his writing system. This meant that not only could speech be recorded verbatim, but anyone with a secret to keep could rest assured that only those in the know would have access to their private notes and correspondence. The man responsible for this was John Byrom, who was born in Manchester in the building still known as The Shambles, in 1692. His system, which he called *The Universal English Shorthand*, became widely accepted and was even taught to students at the universities of Oxford and Cambridge. John Byrom died in 1763, but he is probably best remembered, not for his brilliant invention, but for the hymn he wrote, *Christians Awake, Salute the Happy Morn'*, and the names which he invented and which have come down to us as nursery rhyme characters, *Tweedledum and Tweedledee*.

Meccano: Before the days of computer games, Nintendo, the Wii, X-boxes and the like, kids played with far less complicated toys. And not so long ago, nothing could bring the look of delight to a boy's face on Christmas morning more than the discovery that Santa had brought him a Meccano set. Then, while Mum made the Christmas dinner, Johnny and his dad would spend a few hours of quality time building cars, cranes, models of the Eiffel tower, ships and just about anything else their imaginations could come up with. The only limitation on such creativity was the length of the metal strips or the number of nuts and bolts included in the kit. It was a wonderful toy; it not only amused but it introduced devotees to the principles of mechanics. It was the brainchild of a clerk from Liverpool, Frank Hornby (1863–1936), who first patented his kits as 'Mechanics Made Easy'. He launched his kits in 1901 and at first they were farmed out to an independent manufacturer. Mr Hornby's idea soon caught on in a big way and he found himself having to cope with an ever-increasing demand for his product. To deal with the demand he opened his own factory in Duke Street, near Liverpool city centre. It was also about this time that he began looking for a briefer, punchier name and came up with 'Meccano', and this became the registered trade mark in 1907. The success of the Meccano kits soon outstripped not just demand but Mr Hornby's wildest expectations and so even bigger premises were needed. In 1914 he opened another factory in Binns Road and this was to be the organisation's headquarters until the 1970s. Unfortunately, after the heyday of the 1930s, the world changed; wars, recessions, takeovers, industrial problems and, quite simply, changing tastes all took their toll and, although it is still produced and has thousands of devotees worldwide, Meccano is perhaps no longer the 'must have' toy for the same numbers of today's younger generation.

Frank Hornby also designed and produced the Dinky Toys range and, of course, the Hornby Model Railways which have kept boys (and dads!) happy for hours and even days over the generations. Frank Hornby died a millionaire in 1936; by today's standards he would be classed as a multi-millionaire or even a billionaire.

The Pub Chain: In the early 1880s two brothers from Preston, Simon and Peter Yates, had a bright idea. They could not understand why nobody had thought of offering the working man an opportunity to sample the odd glass of wine, as opposed to beer, at a reasonable price. Until the boys from Preston had their brainwave, wine (including the fortified wines such as sherry and port) had been the preserve of the toffs. Peter and Simon decided to change all that. They were determined to do things properly; no half-measures would be acceptable in building up their business. So Peter trotted off to Spain to study viniculture (well, somebody has to do the hard jobs) and Simon got on a boat and sailed to America to find out all he could about modern business methods. Then they met up again, compared notes, thrashed out the details and, in 1884, opened their first establishment, Yates's Wine Lodge, in Oldham. The success of the venture was beyond their wildest dreams. They probably expected serious opposition

1884

The year of 1884 was an interesting one in the history of drinking in Lancashire. This was the year when Joseph Livesey, the man who dreamt up the idea of the Temperance Movement, which was intended to make us all drink less, died. But it was also the year when the Yates brothers created the pub chain, trying to make us all drink more. Guess who won …

from the hardcore beer drinkers, but no; wines of all types were suddenly popular and within twenty years just about every town in Lancashire had at least one Yates's Wine Lodge. Each such establishment had an almost identical interior layout: the whole area behind the bar was dominated by huge vats of wine, and port glasses and sherry schooners were as common a sight as pint glasses in the more traditional pubs. The atmosphere, even well into the twentieth century, was pure Victoriana and walking through the usually ornate and impressive portals was like travelling back in time.

The Minicar: Those of a certain age will remember a time not so long ago when the three-wheeler car was a familiar sight on our roads. With its tiny engine it put-putted around towns and villages lending a new experience in mobility to people who could not afford a 'proper' car with four wheels. They are no longer manufactured, but their memory lives on in the four-wheel Issigonis-designed 'mini' with which we are all so familiar today. The 'Bond Minicar', as the original three-wheeler version was officially named, was invented by Lawrence 'Lawrie' Bond, an engineer from Preston. He was born in 1907, educated at Preston Grammar School and then spent the war years designing aircraft at the Blackburn Aircraft Company. Just before the end of the war he set up a factory in Blackpool, still designing aircraft, but then moved to Longridge where he concentrated on producing a car intended to be a little run-around for the less well-off. The car was reasonably successful, but it was killed off by the then Labour government's action (or more accurately, inaction).

Tax on three-wheelers was originally far less than that on more conventional cars, but in 1962 the purchase tax rates for both three- and four-wheel cars were equalised and this proved to be disastrous for three-wheelers. The government was asked to re-establish the differential in the taxes but they chose not to and this spelled the end for the three-wheeler. After all, few people would want to buy a three-wheeler when they could buy a four-wheeler for what was now more or less the same price, would they? The last Bond Minicar left the factory in Berry Lane, Longridge, in 1966.

Rugby: Just about every man and his dog knows the story of how the game of rugby was supposedly conceived. A naughty boy who refused to abide by the rules of football, as it was then played, decided to take things into his own hands. He picked up the ball and ran with it as fast as his legs would carry him and – hey presto! – the game of rugby was invented.

The naughty boy who showed such a disregard for rules and regulations was a Lancastrian by the name of William Webb Ellis (1806–1872). He was born in Salford, the son of an army officer and his wife, and went on to study at Brasenose College, Oxford, before deciding to enter the Church. He never married and died in the south of France, where his grave can still be seen in a cemetery in Menton.

The Rugby School memorial plaque reads:

This stone commemorates the exploit of WILLIAM WEBB ELLIS who with a fine disregard for the rules of football as played in his time first took the ball in his arms and ran with it thus originating the distinctive feature of the Rugby game AD 1832

The seismograph: The ancient Chinese are credited with being among the first to invent some sort of early device for giving prior warnings of earthquakes, but the man who devised the first modern seismograph was John Milne (30 December 1850 – 31 July 1913).

Milne was born in Liverpool, although he spent most of his formative years in Rochdale. His family later moved down south and John was educated at King's College School in Wimbledon before going on to study at the Royal School of Mines, which later became part of Imperial College. Once he had graduated, the world became his oyster and, at the tender age of 23, he was receiving tempting offers of employment from all over the globe. One such offer was to take him to the other side of the world, where the government of Japan had offered him the post of Professor of Geology at the Imperial College of Engineering. He arrived there in 1876 and was still living and working there in 1880 when a dreadful earthquake hit the city of Yokohama. His professional interest in earthquakes was aroused and he and his colleagues set about the task of inventing a reliable means of predicting where and when an earthquake was likely to strike and with what intensity. What they came up with is technically referred to as the 'horizontal pendulum seismograph'. The Emperor of Japan was so impressed by John Milne's invention that he bestowed upon him the Order of the Rising Sun (3rd Class) – a rare distinction indeed to be awarded to a foreigner.

John Milne died in 1913 and is buried on the Isle of Wight.

7

LANCASHIRE GRUB

Meals in Lancashire were traditionally substantial. They also have their roots in an age when there was no such thing as a health-and-safety brigade. When the Lancashire hotpot was invented it was a different world. A man would come home on a freezing cold night after a hard day in the mill, down the pit or trying to make the unforgiving earth yield vegetables, or sustain a cattle, and he would want something hot and filling to eat. After a long walk home in the rain or snow he hoped to come in through the front door and be greeted by a smell which offered the promise of a satisfying meal. And, of course, the meal had to be cheap.

Today things are very different. The pits have gone, the mills have disappeared and men and women coming home after a long day at work usually drive up to the front door, possibly pop something in the microwave and then more often than not crash out in front of the telly. Sometimes they might, just for a change, go out to a restaurant where they might be offered some *nouvelle cuisine* creation which is neither filling nor satisfying. And there are establishments in Lancashire which cater for a clientele prepared to pay more and more in exchange for less and less; what is placed on the table in front of these diners often resembles a work of minimalist art rather than a hearty meal. On the other hand, fortunately, there are still places in Lancashire offering traditional Lancashire meals which guarantee satisfaction, that wonderful feeling of contentment and the conviction that all is well with the world.

Fish and chips: There must be few places in Europe, or even the world, where you can't buy fish and chips but the very first chip shop was opened in Oldham, Lancashire, in the 1860s. Within a very short space of time fish was being served with chips, largely due to the invention of the steam locomotive. Before the railways came to this part of Lancashire the fish, landed at coastal towns such as Fleetwood and Morecambe, would have been in a sorry state by the time they reached Oldham. Now the fish could be landed and transported to inner Lancashire within a matter of hours and a short time after that Lancastrians could be tucking into a sustaining and cheap meal.

Nowadays fish and chips sold to take out are wrapped in hygienic, specially prepared paper but not so long ago the outer wrapping was old newspaper. Newspaper had much better insulating properties and it would keep the fish and chips a lot warmer for much longer.

Make your own …

Fish and chips: If you want your fish and chips served the 'proper' way forget all about the spindly French fries (which, incidentally, are probably a Belgian invention, not a French one). The original British chip is chunky and it should be golden brown on the outside and nice and fluffy on the inside.

Have a look at the recipe here:

To make the batter take 8oz of self-raising flour, a pinch of salt and 10fl.oz of cold lager. Put them in a bowl and whisk well until you have a thick, creamy batter.

Nowadays, everything has to be fried in oil, preferably of the vegetable variety. But in the good old days everything, including fish and chips, was deep fried in animal fat, i.e. lard or drippings. If you want to make this dish at home the choice is yours, as both animal fat and vegetable oil can produce excellent results, but for taste the best is probably turkey or goose fat.

Next, the fish. For the traditional version it has to be either cod or haddock, even though chippies offer all sorts of fish that were totally unheard of just a few decades ago. So, take a thick fillet of either cod or haddock, coat in the self-raising flour and put to one side.

Heat the fat or oil until it is very hot. Take the fish and give it a good soaking in the batter before transferring it to the fat or oil. Take care not to get splashed. Cook for no more than ten minutes. Then remove the fish, put it on a warm plate and see to the chips. These should be immersed in the fat and allowed to cook, once again, for about ten minutes.

When the cooking time is up, take the chips out and empty them onto a piece of absorbent paper to get rid of the excess fat or oil and then serve up with the fish, a slice of lemon and salt and vinegar to taste. A serving of peas (or mushy peas) finishes the whole thing off nicely.

Did you know that ...

The slice of lemon traditionally served with fish is not just for decoration? It is there for a supposedly very practical reason. It used to be believed that if someone eating a piece of fish got a bone stuck in their throat the only way to deal with it was to suck on the slice of lemon. In the Middle Ages it was believed that the lemon juice would dissolve the fish bone and thus remove the danger. We would now probably consider this an old wives' tale, but the practice of placing the slice of lemon on the plate has persisted.

During the Second World War, when just about every food you can think of was severely rationed, fish and chips never were?

There is a blue plaque in the Tommyfield Market area of Oldham which claims that it is the 'home of the first British fried chip'? It also claims that all 'fast food industries' can trace their origins back to the first chip shop in Oldham.

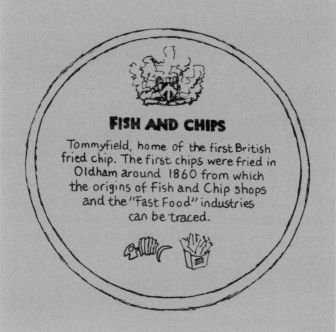

FISH AND CHIPS

Tommyfield, home of the first British fried chip. The first chips were fried in Oldham around 1860 from which the origins of Fish and Chip shops and the "Fast Food" industries can be traced.

Lancashire hotpot: Of all the meals and foodstuffs for which Lancashire is renowned, this has to be the biggie. Even if they have never tasted it, there can be hardly a soul in the whole country who has not heard of it. 'Betty's hotpot' was the staple diet of habitués of the Rovers Return in *Coronation Street* for over fifty years, so fans all over the world will almost certainly have heard of the dish.

There are two main reasons why hotpot was so popular; it was easy to prepare and cheap to make (a third reason was that it was, and still is, delicious!). In the days when Lancashire was a heavily industrialised part of the country and families worked hard all day to keep body and soul together, this was a dish which fitted in perfectly with the demanding chores of the day. A wife could put everything in the pot, place it in the oven and just let it slow cook until evening.

The ingredients are pretty basic: lamb and vegetables (any combination of carrot, onion, potatoes, turnip or leeks) are placed in a deep pot and covered with a final layer of potatoes which have been sliced. In the traditional version there is little or no measuring of the ingredients and whatever is available, in whatever quantities, is thrown into the pot. Stock, or just water, is then added, as well as some seasoning and the whole thing is placed in an oven on a low heat, and left for several hours until ready to eat. It can then be served with beetroot, red cabbage or pickled onions.

As with most traditional meals in life, there are arguments as to which is the 'real' hotpot recipe. In some parts of Lancashire carrots are added, in others they are not; some people make it with beef instead of lamb; some add kidneys but others argue that these would have been an expensive addition to what was essentially a peasant meal. One fairly universal addition, however, is a few good-sized slices of black pudding.

In the past, hotpot might have been accompanied by a glass of inexpensive beer or (and this seems to be mainly a northern habit) a mug of tea. Nowadays (and purists would say this is sacrilege!) Lancashire hotpot can be washed down very nicely with a glass or two of a robust red wine.

Did you know that ...

Lancashire hot pot made without any meat in it is called 'fatherless pie?'

Tripe and onions: This has to be the 'Marmite' of Lancashire dishes; you will either love it or think it is the most revolting thing you could ever see on a plate. Nutritionists tell us that it is very good for us but that probably butters few parsnips with most people. Tripe is usually made from the stomach of a cow, bleached beyond belief to make it look more 'appetising'. You have to have an extremely strong gut to stomach it! At least that's what I think.

There are two kinds of tripe, depending on which of the cow's two stomachs it is taken from and the first stomach (technically known as the rumen) gives us plain tripe: the second stomach (or reticulum) produces the sort that looks as though it is made up of lots of little honeycomb structures and is thus, not surprisingly, known as 'honeycomb' tripe. Aficionados of this particular delicacy eat it cold (i.e. uncooked) with lashings of salt, pepper and vinegar, claiming that it makes a delicious, succulent snack as well as a more than acceptable main meal.

When cooked, especially with onions, tripe is supposed to be delicious and the following is probably the most common way of eating it in Lancashire. If you fancy tasting it, try this:

Take some honeycomb tripe and give it a good wash under running cold water.

Place in a pan of cold water and bring to the boil.

Remove the tripe, cut it into smallish pieces and put back into the pan.

Cut and add three onions, a bay leaf or two and a pint of milk.

Bring to the boil and then allow to simmer for a couple of hours.

Now add a blob of butter and stir gently.

Just before serving, add a sprig of parsley.

Just one tip: if you are thinking of offering this to your friends, make sure you let them know beforehand and have a 'plan B' to fall back on!

Black pudding: Black pudding of one sort or another is found all over the world, so the north west of England cannot claim a monopoly on it. However, among the connoisseurs of such culinary masterpieces, many agree that the champion of champions in the black pudding league is the variety that hails from Bury and in particular from Bury Market.

The essential ingredient of the black pudding is pig's blood. This is gathered into a large vat and mixed with crushed oats, pearl barley, flour, onion and some pork fat which has been chopped into very small pieces. All this is given a thorough mixing before being fed through a machine designed to push it into a lining. In past times the lining was made from the intestines of a pig, but in today's world a bullock's intestine is preferred. It does not really matter though, and what comes out looks like a very fat black sausage.

Not so long ago the black pudding was treated almost like a meal in itself. It could be eaten cold, although most people preferred to heat it up in a pan of boiling water for about twenty minutes, with some mustard spread on it and to eat it just by itself or with bread. Nowadays, however, black pudding is more likely to be cut into slices and fried along with some bacon and eggs … scrumptious!

The pudding

The way we use the word pudding today is not historically correct. The word is now normally applied to the sweet course eaten after the main dish, apart from set expressions such as 'black pudding' and 'Yorkshire pudding', but in fact these are the correct usages. The original pudding was any food which had been cooked in a bag (or a sheep's stomach) and so was very similar to what we would call a sausage. Linguistically, 'pudding' is derived from the Latin for sausage, *botulus*, just as, believe it or not, the potentially fatal infection known as 'botulism'.

Pea soup: This is another winter warmer. It is also another one of those Lancashire dishes that ticks all the boxes: cheap, easy to make, and filling. As the name suggests, the main ingredient for this dish are peas, which grow in such abundance just about anywhere in Lancashire.

How to make it: take half a pound of dry split peas and soak them overnight. The next day, take an onion and a carrot, chop them into small pieces and fry them in a little butter in a saucepan. Now add 4 pints of water and bring to the boil. All you have to do now is add the peas with salt and pepper to taste and the job's done. Just leave it simmering for about three hours. When the time comes, serve it up with chunks of lovely crispy bread and you've got yourself a satisfying meal.

There is, however, an even tastier version, if a little more expensive. For this you need to soak a pound of dried peas overnight. Next morning, put a ham shank or some bacon ribs in a pan of water and boil until the meat is soft and tender. Take the ribs or shank out of the pan but don't throw the water away as this is now your stock and you are going to need it for the next stage. Strip the meat off the bones and cut it into little chunks.

Immerse the peas in the stock, bring it to the boil and then leave it simmering on the stove for an hour or so. At this point you add the meat chunks, together with a carrot or two (chopped into little bits) and let it all simmer away again. You know the soup is ready when the peas take on a mushy, creamy consistency.

Scouse: Until a generation or so ago a kid playing in the streets of Liverpool might suddenly announce that he was not playing any more and was going home. The reason he would give was often 'me mam's made a pan o' scouse.' If he was from one of the very poor districts he would probably be hoping that it wasn't 'blind scouse' – in other words, scouse with no meat in it.

A recipe for scouse:
There are many recipes for scouse and they all claim to be the original. The 'original' concoction as produced by the

Scandinavian sailors was basically just meat, potato and ship's biscuit thrown into a pan and allowed to simmer for a couple of hours. Modern recipes include all sorts of exotic ingredients such as olive oil, thyme and Worcester sauce, few of which would have ever been heard of in a working-class Liverpool house not so many years ago. So if you want to try the ordinary scouse produced by working class mothers trying to feed their family fifty or sixty years ago, try this one:

Half a pound of lamb or beef
A large onion
1lb carrots
5lbs potatoes
1 or 2 Oxo cubes
Salt and pepper
Water

Cut the meat into fairly large cubes and fry in lard or drippings until they are a nice golden-brown colour (I suppose modern cooks will prefer vegetable oil, but for authenticity it has to be lard or dripping).

Now transfer the meat to a saucepan, peel and chop the carrots, onion and potatoes into rustic, chunky cubes. Add the carrots, onions and half the potatoes to the pan, cover with water and add the Oxo cube (or cubes), salt and pepper.

Now put the pan on the cooker and bring everything to the boil. Once the water is boiling turn the heat down and let everything simmer away for about two hours, giving it a gentle stir every now and then. After the two hours add the remainder of the potatoes and allow it all to simmer for another hour or two (depending on taste).

When ready, serve the Scouse on warm plates with a good helping of pickled beetroot, red cabbage or pickled onions. There should be enough with this recipe for between four and six people.

For a slight variant on the above, you might like to try serving the scouse directly onto a thick slice of bread. It's a bit stodgy, but delicious and just the thing to keep you warm on a cold winter's night.

Pie-eaters

In just about every town and village in Lancashire pies of one sort or another form an important, if not staple part, of the normal diet. But the accolade or centre of the pie-eating world has to be Wigan, and in 1992 this honour was formalised by the creation of the World Pie Eating Championship which has been held there every year since.

The reason natives of Wigan are known locally as 'pie-eaters', however, has nothing to do with their dietary preferences. During the General Strike of 1926, when the coal miners of the region went on strike because they rightly felt that they deserved a living wage, the government of the day starved them into submission. They held out as long as they could but were eventually forced to 'eat humble pie', and that is when the nickname 'pie-eaters' was first applied to them.

PUDS AND CAKES

But Lancashire did not only produce substantial, economical savoury dishes. The resourceful housewives of this noble and ancient county have also given the whole country some mouth-watering puds and cakes. Here are just a few:

The Wet Nellie: This used to be a very popular cross between a pudding and a cake in Liverpool as well as the rest of Lancashire. It is very similar to what is known in other parts of the country as 'bread pudding' but there is an important difference: bread pudding will have a more or less standard recipe, but a wet nellie can vary as it's basically a way of using up leftovers. Have a look at this recipe:

One stale loaf of white bread, cut into slices with the crusts removed (stale cake will do as well)
3½oz butter
5oz brown sugar
¾ pint of milk
A handful of dried fruit (raisins, sultanas etc.)
A good shake of mixed spices
3 eggs

Soak the bread in the milk for a couple of hours (or overnight) in a fairly deep tin.

Mix the rest of the ingredients well and pour over the bread. Bake at 180°C until the mixture is springy to the touch (usually about an hour)

When the whole thing is cooked and ready for eating it can be enjoyed warm with custard or ice cream. When cold it can be cut up and eaten just like a slice of cake.

Oh, and by the way, 'nelly' is short for Nelson – the 'official' name for this is a Nelson Cake.

Parkin: This is a delightful cake with a spicy kick to it that sets it just that little aside from sweet confectionary. It is actually found all over the north of England and many Yorkshire people claim that theirs is the genuine article. But Lancastrians claim that they have their own formula which produces a moister, stickier and much tastier end product. The main difference between the two is that in Yorkshire parkin is baked with just treacle, but in Lancashire golden syrup and a bit more sugar are added as well. What Yorkshire and Lancashire have in common, however, is that parkin is traditionally eaten on Bonfire night. Why not give it a go?

8oz oatmeal
8oz self-raising flour
8oz brown sugar
1½ dessertspoonfuls ground ginger
1 beaten egg
4½oz treacle (or molasses)

4½oz golden syrup
A pinch of salt
8oz butter

Put the oatmeal, sugar, ginger, flour and salt into a bowl and mix thoroughly.

Rub in the butter and then add a beaten egg, the syrup and the treacle and give it all another good mix.

Pour into a baking tin and bake for an hour/hour and a half at 160°C.

Eccles cakes: The Eccles cake is simplicity itself. It is a small round cake consisting of flaky pastry wrapped around a handful of currants and topped with sugar. The origin of the sweetmeat is a little obscure, but it seems likely that it all started in a little shop in Eccles on the corner of Vicarage Road and what is now Church Street. This shop was owned by a certain James Birch who, in 1793, thought it would be a good idea to offer them for sale and see what happened. Fortunately for James they were a roaring success; in fact they sold like ... well, hot cakes!

If you have never tried one but are thinking of doing so, don't be put off by some rather unflattering names by which they are known locally. Owing to the density of the currants contained within, they are frequently referred to as 'Flies' graveyards', 'Flies' cemeteries', 'Fly cake' or 'Fly pie'. The currants may look like dead flies, but the concoction is delicious and a real treat for anyone with a sweet tooth.

Here's how to make your own: Take some thin puff pastry and cut into circles each with a 4 inch diameter.

Put 6oz currants in a mixing bowl together with a heaped teaspoon of mixed spice and mix well. Now pour 1½oz of melted butter over the mixture and give it all another good stir.

Take the pastry circles and place a good spoonful of the currant mixture in the centre of each. Pull the edges of the pastry up so that it wraps around the currants completely and seals them in. Place each parcel, now upside down, on a well-greased baking tin. Gently press each cake down with a rolling pin and cut a couple of slashes in the top.

Did you know that ...

In the Wigan area Eccles cakes used to be known as 'slow walking cakes' because it was the custom to serve them to mourners at funerals?

Chorley cakes are almost the same but have added candied peel, use short crust and don't have a sugar topping?

Lancashire cake uses a dough made out of yeast for the casing instead of puff pastry?

Take an egg, beat it and mix with some milk before brushing the mixture over the cakes.

Finish off by giving each cake a good sprinkling of caster sugar and pop it into a moderately hot oven. Approximately twenty minutes later you will have a batch of Eccles cakes to be proud of.

SOME OTHER LANCASHIRE DELICACIES

Parched peas: 'To parch' is an archaic word meaning 'to boil slowly'. In Preston, Bolton and Darwen vendors stand at their little booths in the town centre selling small paper bags or plastic cups full of roasted black peas to which clients can add salt and vinegar to taste. They were traditionally sold in autumn, especially around Bonfire Night.

Butter pie: This seems to be a mainly Preston-based dish and probably has its origins in the city's large Catholic community. It is basically just a meat and potato pie without the meat! Its ingredients are just potatoes, onion and butter and it was traditionally eaten on Fridays when meat was not allowed.

Clapbread: There's not much to this one! It's simply an oatcake made with unleavened dough and cooked on a griddle.

Goosnargh cakes: Named after the little village of Goosnargh, situated a few miles outside Preston, these cakes are really just shortbread biscuits which have had caraway seeds pressed into them before baking. It used to be traditional to eat them on Shrove Tuesday.

The humble nettle

The stinging nettle is a good example of the lengths to which the people of Lancashire were driven, in days gone by, just to survive. When food was scarce, or even non-existent, wives and mothers were driven to extremes in order to feed their families. One of the ways they did this was to make a stew or soup out of nothing but nettles; not because it was the fashionable dish it is in some quarters today, but because there was nothing else available.

On the other hand, the ubiquitous nettle also provided a nice little income for some families who ran their own cottage industry making delicious nettle beer. The area around Heysham was particularly renowned for this in 'the good old days' before it was decided that it was a 'hazard' to the community.

Sad cakes: This is a delicious way of using up the odd bits of pastry left over after making a pie. The bits are gathered up, mixed with a few raisins and then rolled out to make a flat cake which is then baked. When it is cold it can be smeared with butter and eaten as a tasty accompaniment to a nice cup of tea.

Fag pie: Also known as 'fig pie', this was a traditional sweet served up in Lancashire around Easter. As the name suggests, the main ingredient was figs and it used to be served on Mothering Sunday in Blackburn. In Preston, however, it was the tradition to serve it on Palm Sunday. Hence the day came to be known as 'Fig' or 'Fag Pie Sunday'.

There is also a variety of gooseberry known as the Lancashire Lad.

8

NOTABLE LANCASTRIANS

TELEVISION PERSONALITIES

Fred Dibnah (28 April 1938 – 6 November 2004): When Fred died, England lost another of those wonderful eccentrics for which she is famous. With his flat cap and equally flat Lancashire vowels he had charmed and fascinated TV viewers for decades as he demonstrated his unique way of bringing down redundant industrial chimneys. Not for him the instantaneous destruction brought about by dynamite; he much preferred a combination of the painstaking, almost brick-by-brick approach, followed by a huge bonfire at the base, to bring down chimneys that had dominated the skyline around his native Bolton for over a hundred years. He claimed it was a more controllable (and safer) way of getting the job done, and he appears to have been right. It also made for better viewing and was guaranteed to hold people's attention for hours on end. Who could forget the sight of him sounding his klaxon before bringing a towering chimney crashing down and then asking the assembled audience in his Bolton accent, and with a cheeky grin on his face, 'Did you like that?'

But the steeplejacks' steeplejack was not only interested in demolishing industrial eyesores. From childhood he was fascinated by engines and machines and this gave the BBC another opportunity to retain his services and produce high-quality programmes which made for mesmeric viewing.

Even people with no engineering background would sit in front of the TV and watch Fred messing about with traction engines, steam locomotives and other mechanical wonders of a bygone age. He possessed an enthusiasm for things mechanical which communicated itself to his viewers in no small measure.

Did you know that …

Fred was awarded an MBE for his achievements?

He was also awarded Doctorates from Birmingham and Robert Gordon universities?

Professor Brian Cox (b. 3 March 1968): At the tender age of 44 Brian Cox has carved out for himself three professions and has excelled in all of them. He was a successful instrumentalist in a pop band; he became a physicist (and subsequently Professor) at Manchester University; and more recently he has become a regular presenter of scientific programmes on television. This is pretty good for somebody who, by his own admission, did not do very well in his first attempt at A Level maths.

He was born in Manchester, where his parents were both bankers, in 1968 and was educated at the independent Hulme Grammar School in Oldham where he developed an interest in physics and astronomy. However, at the same time he also developed an interest in, and passion for, pop music. By the time he went up to Manchester University his loyalties were, if not divided, then at least divergent. As a student he had to devote at least some of his time to textbooks and the arcane world of particle physics, but also had to find time for playing keyboard with the already successful band D:Ream, whose best-known song was probably 'Things Can Only Get Better', adopted as the Labour Party anthem for the election campaign of 1997. Eventually the band members decided, for one reason or another, that it was time for them to go their separate ways and Brian made up his mind to concentrate on his PhD in Physics. The world of popular music lost a talented instrumentalist, but the world of science (and the TV viewers) gained a gifted and passionate interpreter of the wonders of the universe.

The list of honours that have been showered on Brian Cox is as long as your arm. He is an International Fellow of The Explorers Club and an Officer of the Order of the British Empire. He holds Honorary Doctorates from the Universities of Huddersfield and the Open University and in 2012 he was awarded the Michael Faraday Prize for his unique achievements in communicating the mysteries of astronomy to the rest of us lesser mortals.

He is also a staunch supporter of the Humanist Society.

Kenny Everett (25 December 1944 – 4 April 1995): Born in Seaforth, near Liverpool docks, Kenny Everett (real name Maurice James Christopher Cole) grew up in a staunchly Catholic family and was given a traditional Catholic education. He became a pupil at St Bede's Secondary Modern School in Liverpool and then attended a junior seminary, where he became a choirboy, near York. But the odour of sanctity in which he grew up seems to have had little effect on him and certainly did nothing to stifle his anarchic sense of fun and wicked sense of humour. When he left school his first job was in a bakery but he soon got tired of that. He must have felt that his talents were wasted in a floury atmosphere surrounded by loaves and cakes and decided to take the bull by the horns and apply for a job at the BBC. Unbelievably his cheek paid off and he was offered a job with the Light Programme (the forerunner of Radios 1 and 2), but even more unbelievably turned it down in favour of becoming a DJ on *Radio London* aboard the pirate radio ship, MV *Galaxy*. This could have proven to be a disastrous decision but it turned out not to be; fate must have taken matters out of his hands and decided that his destiny was to be in broadcasting in one form or another. When the government of the day took steps to close down the pirate radio stations, Kenny was employed by BBC TV and radio (frequently hired, fired, and re-hired) and by the independent broadcasting companies as well.

Throughout his career, Kenny Everett displayed a zany wit and 'off-the-wall' humour, much of which depended on an uncanny ability to create characters with humorously apposite names such as the American Army General, Norm Bombthebastards, the radio evangelist Brother Lee Love, the punk Sid Snot, and the Dolly Parton lookalike with the dangerously spooneristic name Cupid Stunt.

Despite his unbelievable genius (or perhaps because of it) he had a disturbed personal life. He was a confessed drug user and an active homosexual at a time when such behaviour was still not acceptable in many sections of the community. Kenny died of AIDS in 1995.

Did you know that ...

Despite Kenny's natural leanings towards anarchy, he was a staunch supporter of the Conservative Party?

Bernard Manning (13 August 1930 – 18 June 2007): Manning was not everybody's cup of tea. His jokes were frequently coarse and, in many people's opinion, in very bad taste. On the other hand, he made a lot of people laugh and carved a career out of offending people on the grounds of race, physical appearance or sexual orientation.

Bernard John Manning was born in Manchester and had a mixture of Jewish and Irish blood in his veins. He left school at the first opportunity and his first job was as an assistant in his father's grocery shop. He then moved on to working in a cigarette factory, before he was called up to do his National Service. The army posted him to Germany where, quite by chance, he discovered a previously unsuspected talent as a performer. Largely out of boredom he took to doing a bit of amateur singing to entertain the troops and this gave him an idea of how he might make a living when he returned home and found himself on Civvy Street again. He served his

Did you know that ...

As part of his National Service duties Bernard Manning stood guard over the Nazi war criminals Rudolf Hess, Albert Speer and Karl Dönitz in Spandau prison in Berlin?

Despite his jokes about Jews he called his own house 'Shalom', the Hebrew for peace?

Esther Rantzen referred to him as 'the villain of comedy'?

apprenticeship as an entertainer in northern working-men's clubs, but his big break came when he was invited to appear on ITV's new show *The Comedians* in 1971. His sense of humour was, however, a bit too close to the bone and as the rising tide of political correctness engulfed the entertainment business, Bernard Manning's appearances on TV dwindled to virtually zero. His jokes and language were far too 'blue' and television producers simply would not risk their own jobs by offering him a slot in their schedules. Jokes about Jews, gas-chambers, cripples, people of Asian and African origin were considered definitely beyond the pale. In his own Manchester club the Embassy, however, it was a case of 'anything goes' and nothing was considered taboo; some people took offence at his brand of humour, but many just took it as he always claimed it was intended, just good fun. But his stage persona was just that, a persona. Off-stage he was known as a generous and clean-living gentleman. He did not smoke, drink, do drugs, was not a womaniser and, as he himself said, never swore in front of his mother.

THE WORLD OF POLITICS

Sir Robert Peel (5 February 1788–2 July 1850): When Robert Peel was born in Bury in 1788 few people would have foreseen the brilliant political career he had ahead of him. Although he was born with the proverbial silver spoon in his mouth he began, at

a very early age, to show that he possessed rare talents and a fine mind. He was educated at Harrow and then went on to Oxford where he graduated with a double first degree in Classics and History. At this point, Robert, and those who knew him, must have realised that his talents would take him far and guarantee success in whatever profession he chose. As it happened, he chose politics and in the cut and thrust of political debate he proved equal to any challenge. As a result his rise was spectacularly meteoric. By the age of 21 he had been appointed Secretary for the Colonies, by 24 he was Chief Secretary for Ireland and then, in 1822, he was appointed by the Duke of Wellington (the Prime Minister) to the post of Home Secretary. It was while he held this office that he implemented policies that had a far-reaching effect on British society for generations to come. He initiated long over-due prison reform and created the Metropolitan Police Force. Originally, the creation of a new police force was a reaction to the terrible problem of crime on the streets of

Did you know that …

'Bobbies' and 'Peelers' take their name from Sir Robert Peel?

He was killed when his horse stumbled and fell on top of him when he was out riding on Constitution Hill in London?

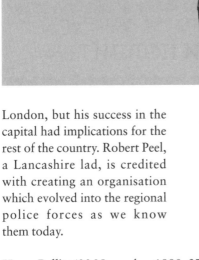

London, but his success in the capital had implications for the rest of the country. Robert Peel, a Lancashire lad, is credited with creating an organisation which evolved into the regional police forces as we know them today.

Harry Pollitt (22 November 1890–27 June 1960): Harry Pollitt is probably only remembered in Britain now by serious students of political or social history, but not so long ago he was a well-known fire-brand fighter for the rights of the working man. He was born in Droylsden, which was then a Lancashire mill town but is now officially in Tameside. His credentials as a member of the working class were impeccable: his father was a blacksmith's striker and his mother a cotton spinner. Both parents, despite a lack of formal education, were politically very aware and instilled in their six children a keen sense of the dignity of honest labour, at the same time as the need to bring about social change and achieve justice for the workers. Harry earned his living as a boilermaker and so knew

the meaning of hard work, graft and sweated toil. He also, at a very early age, became aware of the injustices inherent in a world divided into the bosses and the workers, the exploiters and the exploited.

When the Russian Revolution occurred in 1918, Harry was delighted and the following year took part in the 'Hands off Russia' campaign, a reaction to the western interventionist moves to bring down the Bolshevik government. The government in Russia was not brought down and the newly created Union of Soviet Socialist Republics survived for another seventy years.

Harry Pollitt was a life-long admirer of the Russian revolution and served as General Secretary of the British Communist Party from 1929 till 1956. Despite the revelations of what life in the Soviet Union was really like and Khrushchev's 1956 denunciations of Stalin and the Gulag, Harry Pollitt remained unswerving in his devotion to the cause. A portrait of the erstwhile Soviet leader Joseph Stalin hung on the wall of his living room and Pollitt made it crystal clear to one and all that it was to stay there at least until the day he died.

Did you know that ...

The Soviet Union's leaders were so impressed by the work Harry Pollitt did to further the cause of Communism that they issued stamps with his head on it?

The Soviet Navy also honoured him by naming one of their warships after him?

Harry Pollitt interviewed the author George Orwell when he wanted to enlist in the International Brigade fighting the Fascists in the Spanish Civil War? Accounts suggest that Pollitt took an immediate dislike to Orwell.

Emmeline Pankhurst (14 July 1858 – 14 June 1928): It seems odd to think of it now, but until Emmeline Pankhurst *et al.* came along, women in Britain were not allowed to vote. In a male-dominated world few even considered that woman would want to vote or influence the political life of the country. Eminent Victorians such as Winston Churchill, who was home secretary at the time, firmly believed that women were incapable of exercising political judgement and should stay at home looking after their menfolk and children. It took a determined woman like Emmeline (aided in no small measure by her daughters Christabel, Sylvia and Adela) to change their minds. The Suffragettes, as those demanding voting rights for women became known, fought long and hard to get what they wanted, and several of them, including Emmeline, spent time in prison for using tactics which were deemed by the authorities to be criminal activity.

Emmeline Pankhurst (*née* Goulden) was born in Manchester, the daughter of a wealthy businessman who held radical political opinions. Her mother was also a woman of strong views and was a vehement feminist at a time when such views were hardly the fashion of the day. Emmeline was sent to a Paris finishing school, which her parents had chosen specifically because of the curriculum; the *École Normale Supérieure* offered girls the chance to study 'boys' subjects, such as the sciences, and particularly chemistry. When her education was finished and the time came for her to return to England, Emmeline was a well-educated, elegant young lady. But her feminine refinement hid a steely determination to fight for women's causes in a man's world and this is exactly what she did. Ironically, however, the year (1928) in which she achieved her goal of seeing the vote extended to women over the age of 21, was also the year in which she died.

The Cat and Mouse Game

The prison authorities, no doubt in collusion with the Home Office, took a very hostile attitude to the Suffragettes. If they went on hunger strike they were often force fed. But this was brutal and cruel way of dealing with the problem so another tactic known as the Cat and Mouse approach was adopted. If a hunger striker became so weak it was feared that she might die, she was released from prison. But as soon as she recovered and regained her strength, she was re-arrested and the process began all over again.

THE WORLD OF ENTERTAINMENT

Eric Morecambe OBE (14 May 1926 – 28 May 1984): John Eric Bartholomew was born in Morecambe on the Lancashire coast in 1926. His mother, Sadie, was in love with the stage and was determined that her son should make a career for himself in the world of showbiz. She even took on extra work as a waitress to pay for young John's dancing lessons. She also encouraged him to take part in talent contests, some of which he won. At one contest in 1940, which the young John Bartholomew won, the first prize was an audition with the then famous impresario, Jack Hylton. If he had not performed well the whole thing could have been a terrible disaster and signalled the young lad's ignominious withdrawal from a career on the stage. But it was not a disaster. In fact, Jack Hylton was quite impressed and within a few months the budding performer was on stage at the

Nottingham Empire. It was here that John Eric Bartholomew met Ernest Wiseman, a lad from Leeds, and the two of them immediately struck up a friendship. This friendship developed into a life-long partnership; John changed his name to Eric Morecambe (adopting the name of his home town) and Ernest became Ernie Wise. As 'Morecambe and Wise' the two went on to dominate British television comedy until Eric's untimely death from a heart attack in 1984.

The heart attack that killed him did not come as a complete surprise to those close to Eric. During the war, when he was serving king and country down the mines as a Bevin Boy, he had been discharged as medically unfit for spending his days mining for coal when a medical examination revealed a heart defect. Also, prior to the one that killed him, Eric had had two previous heart attacks and, to make matters worse, he was a heavy smoker.

Eric Morecambe and Ernie Wise (who died in 1999) are probably best remembered for their Christmas shows, which the BBC broadcast at prime time on Christmas Day from 1968 till 1977. These shows drew enormous viewing figures and left their rival programmes standing at the starting gates. Their unique feature was the way in which they ritualistically humiliated their guests, who were usually other 'stars' from the world of entertainment. A particularly favourite butt for their jokes (even when he was not appearing on their show) was the veteran entertainer Des O'Connor. On one memorable occasion Ernie mentioned that Des claimed to be 'a self-made man', to which Eric, quick as a flash, replied, 'Good of him to take the blame.'

Eric Sykes CBE (4 May 1923 – 4 July 2012): This stalwart of British entertainment for over fifty years was born in Oldham, into a working-class family that was no stranger to hardship. Eric's mother died just a few weeks after he was born and his father, a worker in one of Lancashire's myriad cotton mills, had to struggle to make ends meet. Young Sykes's education was minimal but this did not hold him back, although, as he himself would have admitted, sheer luck played an important role in his success. He followed his father into the mills for a while but then, in 1941, Eric enrolled in the RAF where he was trained as a wireless operator. It was while he was 'doing his bit' that he took his first tentative steps in the world of entertainment by performing for his comrades. He also met an officer, Bill Fraser, who not only later became an actor himself, but played a key role in the career of Eric Sykes. Following demobilisation, Eric found himself in London, hungry and down on his luck. By a pure fluke he bumped into his old comrade-in-arms, Bill Fraser, who took him off to a café and gave him a meal. At the end of the meal Bill asked Eric if he would come and work for him as a scriptwriter and after that, the down-at-heel lad from 'up north' never looked back. His natural quick wit, sense of humour and feeling for the absurd meant that writing comedy came naturally to him, and within no time at all he was in demand, writing for other performers and working for the BBC. He then tried his hand at acting and discovered another talent he never knew he had. In brief, a chance meeting on a freezing night in London led to decades of successful work in the entertainment business as a writer, actor and then director, for radio, TV, stage and screen.

There was just one problem. Early in his adult life Eric began to have hearing problems (possibly due to experiencing heavy artillery bombardments during the war) which became progressively worse. He never let it interfere with his work or his zest for life but he did have to learn to cope with his handicap. He learned to lip-read and took to wearing the heavy-duty spectacles that became his trade-mark, even though he did not need them for seeing. They were in fact a disguise for a rather elaborate hearing aid.

Dame Thora Hird (28 May 1911 – 15 March 2003): Critics, biographers and historians of the British world of entertainment usually refer to Thora as 'an institution', and by describing her thus, they are bestowing upon her the highest accolade possible. She not only made an enormous contribution to acting as a profession but never went out of fashion as a consummate exponent of the trade. She never modelled herself on anyone else, but simply and easily assumed whatever personality the role demanded, and then performed it with a gentle mastery that must have been the envy of many in her profession. Her range was enormous: she slipped into the role of the house proud, if mildly domineering, wife and mother in *Last of the Summer Wine*, the over-bearing mother in a comedy series set in an undertaker's premises *In Loving Memory*, and she was stunningly impressive in the performance she gave in *A Cream Cracker under the Settee,* one of Alan Bennett's 'Talking Heads' series of monologues. She could be serious when the role demanded pathos, warm when the role called for a sympathetic character and yet, with a dead-pan delivery, make a humorous role her own. She has gone, but she is certainly not forgotten.

Thora was another of the stars of screen and stage born in Morecambe. Her father was in showbiz; he was manager of the Royalty Theatre in the town and later became involved in organising the entertainments at the end of the pier, so Thora had the smell of greasepaint in her nose virtually from the day she was born. However, she did not make it her first choice when she left school. Her first job was as a cashier in the Co-op, where she worked for ten years, but her natural talents as a performer showed through even here. To relieve what must have been at least a modicum of boredom, she would imitate the mannerisms of her colleagues and then reproduce them in amateur performances at the Royalty as her watchful dad observed and advised.

Thora was enormously successful on the stage, on television, the radio and the big screen, but she never lost the common touch. After a trip to see her daughter and son-in-law, Mel Tormé, in Beverly Hills, she commented that it was 'perfect for a holiday, but there's no corner shop, love'.

Sir Ian McKellen (b. 25 May 1939): Now regarded as one of the finest actors this country has ever produced, Ian McKellen was born in Burnley in 1939. His father was a civil engineer but this was not a profession which convinced the young Ian to follow in his father's footsteps. He showed an early interest in the theatre, which seemed to become even stronger after the family moved to Wigan just after the outbreak of war. No doubt his appreciation of the dramatic was enhanced by the lifestyle the family had to endure over the next few years. Ian would spend his days in school, but then at night, when he was back home within the bosom of his family, he would sleep under an iron dining table which doubled as a mini bomb shelter. When he left school he was offered a place to study English at St Catherine's College, Cambridge, although the pull of the stage was to prove stronger than that of the academic life and he left Cambridge with a 'respectable' degree rather than a good one. After graduating in 1961, Ian made his debut as a professional actor at the Belgrave Theatre, Coventry, where he had been offered a part in a production of *A Man for All Seasons*.

His natural on-stage presence, his wonderfully sonorous voice and impressive acting ability meant that success was merely a matter of time. In fact, within three years of setting out as an actor Ian McKellen was performing regularly in London theatres and earning a reputation as a director also. Accolades and honours were showered on him and in 1979 he was made Commander of the British Empire.

His mastery of the art can be seen in the range of his acting roles. He is a consummate Shakespearean actor who did not consider it beneath his dignity to take on the role of an oleaginous con man in *Coronation Street*, and, of course, few will forget his performance as Gandalf in the film version of *The Lord of the Rings*. Off-stage he campaigns vigorously for causes which he supports with commitment, such as gay rights. He is also a vegetarian and a professed atheist.

Did you know that ...

Sir Ian McKellen rips those pages out of hotel room Bibles which refer to homosexuality as an abomination (Leviticus 20:13)?

Albert Finney (b. 9 May 1936): In 1958 a young, previously unknown screen actor, Albert Finney, suddenly became a household name for his portrayal of Arthur Seaton, a factory worker in Nottingham, whose rough charm and winning smile was a hit with the cinema goers. The film was *Saturday Night and Sunday Morning*, based on the novel of the same title by Alan Sillitoe, and its gritty realism was typical of the 'angry young man' and 'kitchen sink' dramas of the times.

Albert Finney, a bookmaker's son, was born in Salford in 1936. After attending the local schools for his basic education he went on to graduate from RADA and began his career in the theatre where he soon made a name for himself as a fine Shakespearean actor. But after a while he made a foray into films and, after his acclaimed portrayal of Arthur Seaton, he became a box-office hit in his role as the central character in *Tom Jones* (1963). The film enjoyed a degree of success beyond the dreams of those involved with its production, and this might have sealed Albert's career as a film actor, but in fact he preferred to return to the stage. His next major screen appearance was as the Belgian sleuth Hercule Poirot in the film version of Agatha Christie's *Murder on the Orient Express* (1974). He also appeared in two musicals, *Scrooge* and *Annie,* as well as several TV productions, such as *The Green Man* (1990) and *My Uncle Silas* (2001 and 2003). In 2002 he played Winston Churchill in *The Gathering Storm* a role which brought him BAFTA and EMMY 'Best Actor' awards.

Did you know that ...

Albert Finney is not impressed by what he considers to be meaningless honours? He turned down the offer of both a CBE and a knighthood which, he believes, simply serve to perpetuate the class system and snobbery.

For his role in *Annie* (1982) he was paid $1 million, but for his role in *The Duellist* (1977) he was given just a crate of champagne?

He has been nominated for an Oscar five times but has never won one?

Sir Anthony Quayle (7 September 1913 – 20 October 1989):
Anthony Quayle's biography reads like a perfect example of
how art imitates life. In his films he often played the part of an
army officer well versed in the arts of war. In real life he was
a decorated soldier (he rose to the rank of major during the
Second World War) whose exploits were probably every bit as
exciting as anything he got involved with on screen. After basic
training and a fairly routine life as a soldier he was seconded
to the SOE (Special Operations Executive), a unit designed to
carry out acts of sabotage and cause havoc behind enemy lines.
He was parachuted into Albania and spent much of the war
working with partisans, giving the Germans a bit of a headache
and hindering their operations. The problem is, however, that we
do not know very much about what he actually did; it was not a
subject about which he ever spoke, except to give a few sketchy
details. He is thought, however, to have woven a fictionalised
version of his exploits around events in his novel *Eight Hours
from England*.

John Anthony Quayle was born in Ainsdale, near Southport,
into a reasonably well-to-do family (his father was a solicitor)
in 1913 and was educated at a prestigious public school in
Rugby and then at RADA. His interests in the theatre began
early on but were interrupted by the war. On his return to
civilian life he resumed his theatrical contacts and, from 1948
to 1956, directed the Shakespeare Memorial Theatre and was
instrumental in laying the foundations for the Royal Shakespeare
Company.

His first film role was in the 1938 version of *Pygmalion* (for
which he did not even get a mention) yet he went on to become
one of the stalwarts of British cinema. His tall, robust frame
made him suitable for military roles and he appeared in *Ice Cold
in Alex* (1958) and blockbusters such as *The Guns of Navarone*
(1961) and *Lawrence of Arabia* (1962).

Anthony Quayle was knighted in 1985 in recognition of
both his contribution to the theatre and his 'behind the scenes'
activities in the Balkans during the war.

Gracie Fields DBE (9 January 1898 – 27 September 1979): Born Grace Stansfield in Rochdale she became one of the most famous entertainers this country has ever produced. Within a few years of beginning her career she was rich beyond the wildest dreams of just about everybody in England at the time; for an ordinary working-class Lancashire lass she did pretty well for herself. Her singing voice, acting ability, irrepressible cheeriness and no small measure of northern grit all combined to propel her right to the top of her chosen profession.

Gracie was born in a flat above her grandmother's fish and chip shop in a poor area of Rochdale and, like most young girls of her generation and background, seemed destined for a lifelong job in the mills. She did start her working life as a cotton-mill girl, but her performing talents were recognised early on. In 1910, she performed on the stage at the Rochdale Hippodrome and that was that; her life as a mill girl was over and her career as an entertainer had begun.

By 1925 she was appearing at the Alhambra Theatre, London, after which the whole country (if not the world, yet) was her oyster. By the 1930s she had forged a career as a singer, comedienne and actor, and then, when the depression arrived, her ability to cheer people up and raise everyone's spirits became legendary. Her first film *Sally in Our Alley* (1931) made her not merely rich and popular, but super rich and universally popular. And, of course, the film became the vehicle for her song 'Sally', probably the one for which she is still best known.

Did you know that ...

In the 1930s she was paid £200,000 for making just four films? This was an absolutely astronomical sum in those days.

In 1937 she was the highest paid star of the silver screen in the world?

The very last photo of the Hollywood star Bing Crosby was taken in Brighton, England, with Gracie Fields in 1977 just a few days before his death?

When war came in 1939 Gracie was in her villa on the Italian isle of Capri getting over a serious operation she had undergone in Italy and, when she recovered, she soon found herself entertaining the troops in France. In 1940 she married Monty Banks, which was not a good move. His real name was Mario Bianchi, and since he was of Italian nationality they were forced to move to Canada, then USA, otherwise Monty would have been interned as an enemy alien. In 1950 Monty died of a sudden heart attack and two years later 'our Gracie', as she was affectionately referred to, married Boris Alperovici, a Romanian who she maintained was the love of her life.

George Formby (26 May 1904 – 6 March 1961): George was an unlikely success. He had few of the attributes normally associated with a brilliant showbiz career. He was short (5ft 4ins), had a high pitched voice, a toothy grin and was totally dependent on his domineering wife, Beryl. In fact, had it not been for Beryl he probably never would have made it to the top in a world crowded with people who had talent plus good looks. On the face of it, there was just so much about him that should have held him back: in addition to his personal shortcomings he had only minimal schooling, never mastered reading and writing and could not read a note of music. Yet he made it as a singer and musician, playing the banjo (or, strictly speaking, the banjo-ukulele), appealing mainly to his audience's ability to appreciate his sometimes blatantly suggestive lyrics and double-entendres in an age of strict censorship.

Did you know that ...

Even when he was a very rich man, being chauffeur-driven in the most expensive cars of the day, his wife Beryl only allowed him five shillings (25p) a week pocket money?

He was born with a caul which left him blind for the first few months of his life?

Despite his handicaps George became a star in the 1930s and 1940s and was paid amounts of money which were phenomenal when compared to the average working-man's wage. Like Gracie Fields, he was paid more than handsomely to entertain audiences and make them laugh in an age when there was not a lot to laugh about.

He was born George Hoy Booth in Wigan, the son of the music hall entertainer James Booth (who also used the name George Formby as his stage name). As he grew up, young George was sent off to become an apprentice jockey, a calling for which he was well equipped on account of his small stature and slight frame. However, when his father suddenly died, George junior was persuaded to have a go on the stage and audiences took a shine to him right away. He appeared in a host of films, including *Keep Your Seats, Please* (1936), *Let George Do It* (1940) and *Turned Out Nice Again* (1941). He also recorded many songs, most of them with a hint of naughtiness in the words, such as 'When I'm cleaning Windows', 'Leaning on the Lamp Post', 'Why Don't Women Like Me?', 'Imagine Me on the Maginot Line', 'Chinese Laundry Blues', and many, many more.

9

CREATIVE LANCASHIRE

Lancashire might have had a largely industrial and commercial past but that does not mean that no-one in the county had either the time or the inclination to write, paint or compose wonderful music. In fact, the drab cityscapes and harsh conditions of daily life in among the factories and coal mines frequently became a source of inspiration for those who felt that Lancashire life, in all its forms, was worth preserving for posterity. The 'dark satanic mills' provided writers and artists in Lancashire with themes and subject matter which they then fashioned into works of art and literature, comparable with anything produced by the more affluent and leisured parts of the country. Good art and fine literature are not the sole preserve of those fortunates who enjoyed a cosseted childhood; in fact, as Lancashire clearly demonstrates, the opposite is often the case.

WRITERS

Harold Brighouse (26 July 1882 – 25 July 1958): This is probably not a name particularly well known among those who claim to have a good knowledge of English literature, and yet there can be few among the same group who have not enjoyed the 1958 film *Hobson's Choice* starring Charles Laughton and John Mills. It was originally a stage play, written by a lad from Eccles, Harold Brighouse, and tells the story of a patriarchal widower and his three daughters who run a moderately successful shoe-shop business in Salford in the 1880s. Two of the daughters are a little flighty, but the eldest, Maggie, is a hard-headed enterprising woman who realises that the very existence of the business is in the hands (quite literally) of the poorly paid Will Mossop who toils from dawn till dusk in a miserable cellar turning out exquisite footwear. She persuades (or perhaps orders) him to marry her and the couple eventually become the proprietors of the business. Hobson *père* is forced to accept the new situation; his eldest daughter and her husband, his erstwhile employee, now own 'his' business.

The play was first shown on the London stage in 1916 where it was a great success. It was rewritten as a novel by Harold Brighouse's fellow playwright Charles Forrest.

Helen Forrester (6 June 1919 – 29 November 2011): Strictly speaking, Helen Forrester just misses qualifying as a Lancastrian as she was born in Hoylake on the Wirral, but she did spend her formative years in Liverpool and thus can be considered at least an honorary Scouser and Lancastrian. She also wrote about where she grew up in ways which guarantee her a place in Liverpool's literary annals of that fair city, although anyone who reads it will be struck by the relentless descriptions of poverty and hardship that were the normal lot of many residents in the 1930s. The title of her first novel, *Twopence To Cross The Mersey*, was a reference to the fare on the ferry from Liverpool to Birkenhead. This work also summed up the dire poverty in which her family (and many others) lived. In fact neither she nor her mother had the two pence (less than one penny in today's money) to pay for the young Helen to catch the ferry to visit her grandmother on the Wirral. It has been claimed that Helen's novel was the first of the 'misery' novels that are so much in vogue today.

She was born into a middle-class family in Hoylake and was brought up in relatively affluent surroundings in the south of England where her father was a businessman. But when her father lost his job the family's world fell apart; they could no longer afford to live in the more affluent south and within a short space of time found themselves in a rented flat in the

Toxteth area of Liverpool. Helen, at the tender age of 11, was taken out of school and had to look after her younger siblings. Few who read her books could fail to be impressed with the way she coped with the burden of responsibility that was so suddenly and unexpectedly thrust upon her young shoulders.

Anthony Burgess (25 February 1917 – 22 November 1993): The term 'Renaissance Man' could almost have been invented to describe Anthony Burgess. His talents appear to be endless and his accomplishments many: he was a brilliant writer, a talented musician and an extremely competent linguist. He spoke French, Spanish and German and taught himself Farsi (Persian) well enough to translate T.S. Eliot's *The Waste Land* into the language. He also gained a good knowledge of Malay while teaching in the Far East, and used his knowledge of Russian to invent teen slang in the novel (and film) for which he is perhaps best known, *The Clockwork Orange*.

John Anthony Burgess Wilson was born in the Harpurhey area of Manchester into a relatively well-off family living in a very poor area. He originally intended to study music at Manchester University but was refused a place, unbelievably, because his physics exam results were so poor! Undaunted, he studied English instead and then went on to write some of the greatest contributions to modern English literature, including *Earthly Powers* which, many critics agree, was his finest novel.

Alfred Wainwright (19 January 1907 – 20 January 1991): Born in Blackburn, Alfred grew up in a family beset with straitened circumstances. His father was a stonemason and probably could have earned a decent wage, but his fondness for the bottle put a constant strain on the family finances. At the age of 13 Alfred left school and was taken on by Blackburn Borough Engineers' Department as an office boy, but soon made up his mind that he wanted to 'get on in the world'. He studied at night school and eventually qualified as an accountant and was so good at his job that from 1948 until 1969 he became Borough Treasurer for Westmorland, based in Kendal, having fallen in love with the Lake District and moved there in 1941.

His passion for the lakes and fells of what is now Cumbria bordered on the obsessive. He spent years tramping up hills and down dales at every possible opportunity, before he immortalised his love affair with that part of England by writing seven *Pictorial Guides to the Lakeland Fells*. This was a labour of love that took him thirteen years to complete. His handwritten manuscripts and beautiful sketches were first published by the *Westmorland Gazette* and were an immediate success with the newspaper's readers. Publication in book form soon followed and the reaction among readers and publishers alike was astounding. Just about everyone spotted the work of a genius and even today, sixty years after the first guide was published, they are still recognised as by far and away the best available walking book to 'fellwanderers' (Wainwright's term), be they of the serious or occasional kind.

ARTISTS

L.S. Lowry (1 November 1887 – 23 February 1976): L.S. Lowry is probably best known to most people for the simplicity and, at first sight, unsophisticated style which characterises his paintings. The landscapes and backdrops he prefers are the grim (and, in many cases, grimy) streets surrounding the mills, factories and coal mines of his native Lancashire. The people who inhabit this world appear dehumanised as Lowry depicts them making their way to and from their smoky homes and places of work. These 'matchstick men' (and women), as they have been called, seldom show any individuality; they exist merely to keep the wheels of industry in motion and it is the wheels of industry that keep them in their place. Most of the men who feature in his paintings appear downcast, plodding along with their hands in their pockets and their heads bowed, utterly resigned to a dismal life from which they can never escape. Nor do they even appear to ever think of escape. Works such as *Going to Work; The Bandstand, Peel Park, Salford; The Mill Gates* and *Industrial Landscape, Ashton-under-Lyne* illustrate perfectly how Lowry saw the relationship between the individual and his industrialised environment.

Laurence Stephen Lowry was born in 1887 in Stretford, near Manchester. As a child he was something of a loner who harboured a secret fascination with art that was not appreciated by his parents. At school he proved to be less than gifted academically and left at the first opportunity to become a clerk (and later a rent collector) in a property management company. But when he wasn't collecting rent or checking the rent books he took private painting lessons and was eventually accepted into the Manchester School of Art (now absorbed into Manchester Metropolitan University) where he studied under the French impressionist Pierre Adolphe Valette. But he never became a full-time professional artist; he worked for the Pall Mall Property Company in Manchester right up to his 65th birthday and did all his painting in the evenings and at weekends.

He died in 1976 and is buried in Chorlton-cum-Hardy cemetery in Manchester.

Did you know that ...

Lowry never considered himself to be a 'proper' artist? He said, 'I am not an artist. I am a man who paints.'

George Stubbs (25 August 1724 – 10 July 1806): George Stubbs was born in Liverpool and was fascinated all his life by anatomy. As a young man he followed in his father's footsteps and became a currier, preparing animal hides and turning them into the polished leather needed by manufacturers of saddles, gloves, boots and shoes. But when his father died there were great changes in George's life. He was apprenticed for a brief time to learn the engravers' trade but this was not for him. He upped sticks and moved to York in the 1740s where he was able to study anatomy at the Count Hospital. His studies were not in vain and he published a textbook on midwifery, before travelling to Rome to study the *modus operandi* of the great Italian painters. When he returned to England he settled down for a while in Lincolnshire (1754) where he began a detailed study of the horse. With the help of a newly acquired lady-friend he dissected horses' carcasses and thus gained a detailed knowledge of their bone structure and muscle function. All this, of course, was of inestimable help to observations of horses and how they move. In 1766 he published *The Anatomy of the Horse*.

However, at the same time as studying and writing books, George was also acquiring a reputation as an artist among the aristocracy. The upper echelons of society (including dukes, marchionesses, not to mention the Prince of Wales) commissioned him to produce works with which they no doubt intended to adorn their grand houses, and Stubbs the artist did not disappoint. He painted exotic animals (lions, tigers, etc.) as well as wonderful pastoral images of village life and family groups. But the paintings for which he is mainly remembered are those of the horse; *Whitejacket,* probably his most famous painting, now displayed in the National Gallery, is a stunning depiction of a prancing horse. With photographic accuracy George captured the fleeting moment of a horse on its hind legs and, with the keen eye and delicate brush of a gifted artist, brought the whole thing to life. Few artists have managed to capture this noble animal on canvas with such skill.

MUSICIANS

Eddie Calvert (15 March 1922 – 7 August 1978): Eddie Calvert was a household name and extremely successful entertainer before the pop world was taken over by the 1960s groups. He was known as 'the man with the golden trumpet', and not without reason. Even people who were not particularly impressed with trumpet music had to admit that Eddie had something special and could make a trumpet do things that few other exponents of the instrument could manage or would even attempt. In the 1950s this was the man who more or less dominated the music scene, and his renditions of *Lili Marlene, Cherry Pink and Apple Blossom White* and the tune for which he is probably best known, *Oh Mein Papa,* have guaranteed him a place in the pantheon of British entertainers.

Albert Edward Calvert was born in Preston, the son of a cobbler (some sources say 'master boot maker') who was also a passionate musician and brass bandsman. Music, and particularly trumpet playing, was in Eddie's blood from the cradle and as soon as his little hands were big enough to hold a trumpet he started learning how to play. There was no question of his having to be coerced into practising; he proved to be a willing student and within no time at all he was demonstrating a precocious talent as a player. In fact, he was so good that he played for the Preston Town Silver Band when he was still a child and was the band's soloist by the age of 11.

During the Second World War, Eddie was called up and joined the Tank Regiment. However, he was involved in a motorcycle accident which left him unfit for service for a while. By the time he had recovered, the authorities had decided that, with his musical talents, he could serve his country better by entertaining the nation and bolstering morale. This meant that when he was demobbed his future was already mapped out for him. In peace time he merely continued what he had been doing in war time and very soon the royalties were pouring in. By the 1960s, however, musical tastes had changed and interest in his kind of music waned. At the same time, Eddie was becoming more and more disenchanted with Britain's political leaders and he decided to go and live in South Africa. He died of a heart attack in Johannesburg in 1978.

William Walton (29 March 1902 – 8 March 1983): Next time you watch *The Battle of Britain* on the telly and find that the music is as exciting as the dog-fight aerobatics of the RAF and Luftwaffe pilots, remember that you have a Lancashire lad to thank for the patriotic stirrings in your soul! Much of the music was scored by Sir William Walton who was born in Oldham in 1902 into a family of gifted musicians who encouraged the young and obviously talented William to follow his musical instincts. He went up to Oxford University to study music when he was only 16, and although he left without taking his degree, enjoyed a highly successful career as a composer.

When he left Oxford he soon found himself hob-nobbing with the literati of the day; the Sitwells took him under their wing and probably influenced his literary interests and musical development. It was at about this time that William discovered jazz and was intrigued by its musical possibilities. In the 1920s, when money was a bit tight, he was able to keep body and soul together by playing the piano in London jazz clubs.

But his real love was classical music and so, while jazz paid the bills, William was composing the symphonic and choral music which sealed his reputation as a serious musician.

When he met the Hungarian-born film producer and director Paul Czinner, William's career path took him in yet another musical direction and he produced four film scores, including the music for *As You Like It* (1936). Later on he was invited by Sir Laurence Olivier to produce scores for the films *Henry V* (1944), *Hamlet* (1948) and *Richard III* (1955).

What is not generally realised, however, is that when he came to compose the score for *The Battle of Britain* (1960) he would soon find himself embroiled in a real-life drama of his own. When the score was finished and he presented it to the film company they were not overly impressed. In fact, they rejected most of it and invited Ron Goodwin to come up with an alternative score. Understandably, this caused a certain amount of friction (Lawrence Olivier threatened to walk out) and a compromise had to be found; both scores were used in a happy *mélange* in what appears to be a seamless musical combination. The result was that when we watch the film now, it is difficult if not impossible for most people to know when they are listening to Walton's music and when they are listening to Goodwin's. The film credits attribute the music to both composers, but no clue is given as to who did which bits.

Sir William Walton left Britain and spent the last days of his life with his wife on the island of Ischia, off the coast of southern Italy.

Robert Lockhart (26 March 1959 – 23 January 2012): The son of a baker (and gifted amateur pianist) and a hair dresser, Robert was born in Wigan and grew up to be one of the most productive musicians this country has ever produced. His catholic tastes and natural versatility meant that he was at home both as a composer and performer in any musical environment ranging from a classical orchestra to a modern rock combo. Nor was he by any means out of his comfort zone playing in a jazz band.

He left Oxford with a double first in music in 1979 and then continued his studies at The Royal College of Music, although he was simultaneously in great demand as a performer and gave regular piano recitals and venues all over the country and on *Radio 3*. But he had a change of heart and decided that his main area of expertise was to be composing rather than performing, and from 1986 to 1989 he was Musical Director at The Royal National Theatre and composed many scores for the West End and for Broadway. He also found time to produce scores for TV; he composed the music for BBC's *Inspector Lynley* series, ITV's *The Safe House, Grafters* and *The Bullion Boys* to name but a few.

Music was an obsession with Robert Lockhart, but he also had a passionate relationship with cigarettes and alcohol. He was a *bon viveur* and liked nothing better than belting out tunes at a party with some lissom female draped over the piano. Unfortunately, his hell raising took its toll and was probably a contributory factor in the health problems that plagued him in middle age. He was diagnosed with cancer and underwent major surgery from which he seemed to recover and was able to start composing again. He died of a heart attack at the cruelly young age of 52.

FILM ANIMATOR

Nick Wulstan Park (b. 6 December 1958): Nick Park was born in Preston on the Greenlands Estate, but the family later moved out to the tiny rural Lancashire village of Walmer Bridge. Nick's father was an architectural photographer and no doubt was able to pass his interest in things artistic and his fascination for still and moving figures and images. Certainly, by the age of 13 Nick was already displaying an unusual gift for art and was taking a keen interest in film animation. When the time came to move on to university he enrolled in the Communication Arts course at what is now Sheffield Hallam University. His next academic port of call was the National Film and Television School and it was while studying here that he began working on *A Grand Day Out,* his first film featuring the characters for which he is now famous all over the world, Wallace and Gromit.

Almost as soon as he left college, Nick Park was visited by astounding success. He worked for a while as an animator in Bristol and then began producing animation-based advertisements for TV, some of which were universally recognised as the best ever seen on the small screen. In 1993 he returned to his beloved Wallace and Gromit figures and breathed life into them in *The Wrong Trousers*, which was then followed by *A Close Shave* in 1995. In 2000 he produced *Chicken Run,* a feature-length animation film which brought him huge acclaim among critics and public alike. In 2005 his film *Wallace and Gromit, the Curse of the Were Rabbit* won him the 'Best Animated Feature Oscar' at the 2006 awards ceremony.

Did you know that ...

In 2007, Nick Park was commissioned to produce a bronze stature of Wallace and Gromit to be placed in a prominent position in his home town of Preston?

Saint Wulstan (aka Wulfstan) who lived from 1008 to 1095 was the only Saxon bishop to survive the Norman invasion. He is also the patron saint of vegetarians.

CARTOONIST

Bill Tidy (b. 9 October 1933): Although Bill was born in Birkenhead he is quite entitled to call himself an adopted or honorary Lancastrian, as he grew up in Liverpool where his mother had an off-licence shop. As a boy, Bill Tidy attended St Margaret's School in Anfield and when his formal education finished he took a job in one of Liverpool's many shipping offices. But in 1952 he decided that he wanted to do more than sit in an office all day and so he joined the army and signed on with the Royal Engineers. At that time, when Britain still had her empire, the Forces offered fit young men an opportunity to see the world which would otherwise have been denied them. So Bill packed his kitbag and went off to serve queen and country in places such as Germany, Korea and Japan. It was in Japan that Bill's career veered off in an unexpected direction. He had always been a gifted (but untrained) artist and while he was in Japan he sold one of his cartoons to an English-language newspaper and the rest, as they say, is history. When he returned to the UK he worked for an advertising agency in Liverpool, producing little sketches and drawings of greenhouses to accompany advertising slogans in the *Radio Times*. But he soon discovered that he could make a lot more money as a freelancer selling drawings to newspapers under his own name. In 1957 he took the plunge and decided to become a full-time professional cartoonist.

Pretty soon Bill was making a reasonable living from his witty cartoons and his output was prodigious; by 1966 he was producing something like fifteen completed drawings a day and was by now a household name. He was in great demand to churn out cartoons for magazines and newspapers such as *Private Eye* (*The Cloggies*) and *The Daily Mirror* (*The Fosdyke Saga*) which was adapted in 1983 as a long-running series for BBC Radio 2 and which Bill wrote in conjunction with John Junkin. Other publications which benefitted from Bill's talent include *The New Scientist, Datalink, Today, The Mail on Sunday, The Yorkshire Post, Punch* and many more. In addition to all this, Bill Tidy has found time to write over twenty books and produce the illustrations for more than seventy.

He was awarded the MBE in 2000 'for Services to Journalism'.

10

SPORTING STARS

Lancashire is 'not behind t' door' (old Lanky expression) when it comes to sport. The annals of sporting histories are peppered with the names of footballers, cricketers rugby players etc. who were nurtured by the fertile Lancastrian soil and did both their county and country proud.

FOOTBALLERS

Sir Tom Finney OBE (b. 5 April 1922): Tom Finney was born in the Deepdale area of Preston and went on to become one of

the finest footballers the country has ever seen. His father was a plumber and he insisted that his son should learn the trade before he signed on as a professional footballer. He took his father's advice, qualified as a plumber and was consequently nicknamed 'The Preston Plumber' all the time he played for Preston North End. He was a prolific goalscorer and a great ambassador for the sport. Any visitor to the city today will not go very far without being reminded of one of Preston's greatest sons: there is a road, a pub and a school for special needs children named after him. He also played for England, scoring memorable goals against Italy in 1947 and the now defunct Soviet Union in 1958.

During the Second World War, Finney served with 'Monty' (General Bernard Montgomery) in the 8th Armoured Corps in North Africa.

Nat Lofthouse OBE (27 August 1925 – 15 January 2011): Nat Lofthouse played for the Bolton Wanderers for his whole career and was capped thirty-three times playing for England. He was born in Bolton and was a keen footballer almost from the day he learned to walk. He found himself playing for Bolton's first eleven at the age of 14 and even scored two goals against Bury in his very first match. In 1952 Nat Lofthouse earned the nickname 'The Lion of Vienna' because he scored twice playing for England in a match against Austria, despite some very rough treatment and tackles (some would say fouls) from the opposing side. In 1953 he was named English Footballer of the year.

Bolton Wanderers

The club was founded in 1874 by the Revd Thomas Ogden and its members played on land adjoining a church on Deane Road. Unfortunately, a couple of years later there was something of a disagreement between the vicar of the Deane Road church and the team members and the result was that they were not allowed to use the church facilities again. In other words, they found themselves 'homeless' and had to play their 'home' matches at various grounds as and when they became available. In recognition of the fact that they were now of no fixed abode they adopted the name 'Bolton Wanderers' in 1877.

Nat served his country in the war as a Bevin Boy, enduring harsh and sometimes positively dangerous conditions as a coal miner at the Mosley Common mine near Wigan.

Sir Geoff Hurst MBE (b. 8 December 1941): Geoff Hurst was born in Ashton-under-Lyne and although he and his family moved down to Chelmsford in Essex when he was only 8, he is still claimed by Lancastrian football fans as one of their own.

Geoff will always be remembered for one of the goals which he scored (or did not score) against West Germany in the 1966 World Cup final. At the time, the German side maintained that the ball had not crossed the goal line and therefore should not have been allowed. Although England won 4–2 after extra time, there are those who believe that Hurst's third goal hit the crossbar and fell onto the goal line itself and so, technically speaking, did not land inside the West German goal. The argument will probably continue among the aficionados of the game for many years to come.

As things stand at the moment the records make it clear that the referee and linesman both believed that a goal had been scored and this gives Sir Geoff Hurst his other claim to fame: he is the only footballer ever to score a hat-trick in a World Cup final.

Wayne Rooney (b. 24 October 1985): Wayne Rooney grew up in a council house in the Croxteth area of Liverpool. His passion for football was evident from an early age and by the time he was 9 he was already a member of the Everton FC Academy. By his mid-teens he was playing professionally and making his mark in no uncertain fashion on the game at the highest level. If reports are to be believed, he is now one of the most highly paid players in the history of the sport, earning an estimated £1 million a month. He originally played for Everton but in 2004 signed on for Manchester United and has been a member of the England squad since 2003, when he became the youngest-ever player in the England side since 1879. To date, he has represented England seventy-nine times and has scored thirty-three goals.

Manchester United

It seems almost incredible now but the mighty Man United began life in 1878 as the obscure Newton Heath LYR Football Club. The initials LYR stood for 'Lancashire and Yorkshire Railway' and formed part of the team name because the players all came from the company's Carriage and Wagon department. When the team was formed the intention was probably just to give the lads something to do at weekends or on days off, and most of their matches were played against other LYR departments or the employees of other private railway companies. Their first league match was against Bolton Wanderers on 20 November 1880 when they were subjected to a humiliating 6–0 defeat. Fortunately for today's team (and fans) their on-pitch skills have improved a bit since then.

Wayne Rooney's career at Manchester United has been spectacular. Nobody could doubt the magnificent contribution his goalscoring talents have made to his team's success, both at home and on the international scene. Nor can there be any doubt that future generations will look back on his career as one of the most dazzling in the whole history of 'the beautiful game'.

CRICKETERS

Cyril Washbrook CBE (6 December 1914 – 27 April 1999): When Sir John Major (a passionate cricket fan) became prime minister in 1991, one of the first things he did was award Cyril Washbrook a CBE. The award was long overdue and his achievements dated back almost sixty years – it is amazing that it took so long but at least Cyril's contributions to the game have finally been recognised.

Cyril Washbrook was born in Barrow, just outside Clitheroe, and took to cricket like a duck takes to water. In the 1930s he was playing for Lancashire and England as a right-handed batsman, but it was in the late 1940s (after serving as a PT Instructor in the

RAF during the war), that he really showed what he was made of. He scored six Test centuries in matches against Australia, New Zealand, the West Indies and South Africa. In 1954 he was appointed Lancashire's first professional captain and became a Test selector in 1956.

By the time he came to retire in 1959 he had played 500 matches for Lancashire and scored a massive total of 34,101 runs. If the war had not interrupted his playing career, who knows what magnificent achievements he would have managed. The consensus among the cricketing fraternity is that they would have been glorious.

Frank Holmes Tyson (b. 6 June 1930): Officially classed as having been a right-arm fast bowler, this description of Frank Tyson falls somewhat short of capturing the true nature of his bowling prowess. He was one of the fastest bowlers the sport has ever seen and, in the 1950s, was dubbed 'Typhoon Tyson' by an admiring press pack who were totally in awe of the power in his right arm. Don Bradman, the Australian cricketing legend, described Tyson as the fastest bowler he had ever seen and when, in the 1954/55 season, England beat the Aussies three Tests to one, the victory was due in no small measure to Tyson's speedy deliveries.

Frank Tyson was born in Farnworth, near Bolton, and as a boy spent hours playing cricket and practising his bowling against his brother David. His playing career (for Lancashire and England) was relatively short (but extremely impressive!) and he emigrated to Australia in 1960. He continued to be involved in the game which he loved as a coach and commentator, but at the same time followed his other, more academic interests. He was a graduate in English from Durham University but also had a keen interest in Modern Languages. Unsurprisingly, he chose a second career which would allow him to indulge these interests and became a schoolmaster at a grammar school in Melbourne, where he eventually became Head of the Languages Department. He is now fully retired but still leads an active life and, in his own words, just enjoys waking up every morning to be greeted by the sun.

The Hat-Trick

We have cricket to thank for the term 'hat-trick'. It was first used in 1856 when a leading cricketer of the day, H.H. Stephenson (cricketer and cricket coach at Uppingham School in Rutland), bowled out three opposing batsmen with three balls during a match in Leicestershire. To mark this achievement, the players had a whip-round and presented Stephenson with a hat (or it might have been a cap) which had been bought with the money. The practice of collecting money to mark similar outstanding sporting achievements has now been dropped, but the expression 'hat-trick' has not only survived but has now spread to other sports as well. In football, a 'perfect hat-trick' is achieved when a player scores one goal with his right foot, one with his left and a third from a header.

Andrew 'Freddie' Flintoff MBE (b. 6 December 1977): Andrew Flintoff is what is known in cricketing circles as an 'all-rounder', meaning that he is competent in all three of the game's disciplines: bowling, batting and fielding. He made his first appearance as a first-class cricketer in 1995 when, playing for Lancashire, he took his first steps to stamping his mark on the game. Primarily a batsman, he could also intimidate the opposition by bowling a ball towards a batsman at an astonishing speed of 90mph. Like Frank Tyson's, his career as a cricketing representative of both his county and country was relatively short. Nevertheless, he too made a tremendous impression on those who played against him, with him or just watched him from the side lines. The list of awards showered upon him has been awe-inspiring: in 2005 alone he was awarded an MBE, selected as PCA Player of the Year, BBC Sports Personality of the Year and ICC Player of the Year.

Since retiring from full-time cricket Flintoff has carved out for himself a career in TV and embarked on several business initiatives. He has also, almost unbelievably, made the transition from the first-class cricket pitch to the boxing ring. He had his first professional fight as a heavyweight in November 2012 and defeated his American opponent, Richard Dawson, on points.

Outside the ring and off the cricket pitch Freddie has done an enormous amount for charity and to date has raised over £1 million for disabled children.

He also features in the *Guinness Book of Records* for popping the greatest number of party-poppers in one minute.

Brian Statham CBE (17 June 1930 – 10 June 2000): When Brian Statham died in Stockport in 2000, Lancashire and England cricket lost a player who, like his contemporary 'Typhoon Tyson', was up among the finest the game had ever seen. He played seventy test matches for England between 1951 and 1965 and, by the time he retired, had taken an unbelievable 2,260 wickets. The famous cricket pundit E.W. Swanton claimed that Brian was the greatest all-rounder Lancashire had ever produced.

John Brian Statham was born in Gorton, Manchester, and was a devotee of cricket from an early age, practising with his

three brothers who were just as mad about the game as he was. Curiously, when he was accepted into the world of professional cricket, he immediately acquired the soubriquet 'George', which stuck with him for the rest of his professional life. The reason he was rechristened by his team members was simply that the Lancashire side had not had anyone called George for some time and thought they should have. Brian was chosen as the lucky candidate to bear the illustrious name and it would appear that he had little say in the matter.

Another curious fact about 'George' was that when he first turned up to play for Lancashire, he had never had any formal coaching in cricket. His talent was completely natural; as soon as he picked up a bat and ball as a young boy he seemed to know what to do with them. All that was needed was a bit of practise and once he made his professional debut it was not long before both players and pundits were sitting up and taking a great deal of notice of this gangly youth. At a Roses match in 1950 he almost single-handedly demolished the Yorkshire batsmen, seeing off the first three batsmen for just three runs! But it was in the West Indies during the 1953/54 tour that he really showed what he was capable of: he dismissed Worrall, Walcott and Stollmeyer (all legends in the world of cricket) for ten runs. There can be few bowlers who can claim to have matched that.

RUGBY PLAYERS

When the young lad from Salford disobeyed all the rules by picking up the ball and running towards the opposing team's goal, little did he imagine the legacy his actions would leave. His dash down the pitch created a game which spread all around the world like wildfire. It is now played in places as far apart as Wales and Tonga, France and Australia, New Zealand and South Africa and even Italy has recently discovered the excitement that can be aroused by big men bashing into each other and chasing an odd-shaped ball up and down the pitch. Just like any other sport, the game of rugby has produced its stars, many of whom are native Lancastrians.

William 'Bill' Blackridge Beaumont CBE (b. 9 March 1952):
Anyone old enough to remember the 1970s and '80s will have
heard of Bill Beaumont. Even non-sporting types, so long as they
watched a bit of television or read a newspaper, could not fail to
have heard of this sporting legend. His giant frame and prowess
on the rugby field made him one of the dominant personalities in
sport throughout the world. He regularly featured on the back
pages and was also frequently seen on the small screen.

He was born in Chorley, the great-great grandson of Joseph
Hargreaves, the man who, in 1888, founded what was to become
the Beaumont family business. Bill went to school in Kirkby
Lonsdale and Ellesmere College in Derbyshire, before he began
an almost schizophrenic existence, earning a living working and

learning the ins and outs of the family textile business whilst also training for and playing rugby. He played rugby for his native Lancashire, learning his craft as a member of the Fylde Rugby Club which has its HQ at Lytham St Annes. The list of honours he accumulated over his career is singularly impressive: he won thirty-four caps playing for England (twenty-one of them as captain); he is vice-chairman of the International Rugby Board and is chairman of the Rugby Football Union. For many rugby fans, however, he had two moments of glory. The first was in 1979 when, as captain of the North of England team, he led it to victory over the All Blacks who, at the time, were considered to be almost invincible. The second was a year later, in 1980, when he guided the England team to their first Grand Slam triumph in twenty-three years.

Francis Edward Cotton (b. 3 January 1947): Known to most people as 'Fran', Francis Cotton was born in Wigan and attended Newton-le-Willows Grammar School before moving on to study at Loughborough University where he graduated with a degree in Physical Education and Mathematics.

During his rugby career Fran played for Sale, Coventry RFC and Lancashire and the British and Irish Lions. He was also selected to play for England and played his first international match against Scotland in 1971. All in all, he played for England thirty-one times and captained the side three times.

In 1977 Fran acquired the nickname 'Mudman', on account of the keen eye of a press photographer, Colin Elsey. A former rugby player himself and co-founder of the magazine *Coloursport,* he caught a glimpse of Fran emerging from a gladiatorial skirmish covered in mud and glory and snapped him. It was (and still is) a wonderful photograph as it sums up the animal power and elemental nature of the game and is now widely recognised as being one of the finest sporting photos ever taken.

In 1997, Fran was appointed tour manager for the British Lions. When he retired in 1980 he went into business, setting up clothing firm Cotton Traders, but has always maintained his links with the game he loves. He was elected to the Board of Sale Rugby Club in 2007.

William John Heaton Greenwood MBE (b. 20 October 1972):
Known to most people just as Will Greenwood, he was born in
Blackburn and acquired a taste for the game as a child, vigorously
encouraged by his father, Dick, who was also a passionate rugby
player. As an amateur Will played for Preston Grasshoppers and
the famous Merseyside team, Waterloo RFC. When he turned
professional he played for Harlequins, Leicester Tigers, England
and the British and Irish Lions.

Will Greenwood, a native Lancastrian, was educated over
the border in Cumbria at the prestigious fee-paying Sedburgh
School which has an almost unequalled tradition of producing
world-class rugby players. In fact, the school achieved a
certain degree of immortality on 8 April 1993 when a rugby
ball, bearing the school's name, was carried into orbit on the

Football and Rugby Balls

The balls used in both rugby and football have changed
considerably since the games were first played. The strange fact
is, however, that the 'odd' rugby ball is not odd at all and it is
probably the football that has changed its original shape. In the
early days of both games the ball was actually an inflated pig's
bladder covered with leather strips to prevent it from bursting the
first time it was given a hefty whack by a size nine boot. It was not
until the mid-nineteenth century that the bladder was replaced by
rubber, a development which allowed the shape to be determined
by the requirements of the game. In football a purely spherical
shape was chosen, as it had a more predictable bounce and was
easier to direct when it was being kicked along the ground. But in
rugby, where players pick the ball up and run with it held close to
the upper body, it was decided to keep more or less to the original
bladder shape.

But the pig's bladder ball is not dead! It is being reborn in
Lancashire. In 2012 the artist John O'Shea, in conjunction with
Liverpool University's Clinical Engineering Department, launched
the Pig's Bladder Football movement, the aim of which is to 'grow'
pig bladders from cells under laboratory conditions. These will
then be used to make footballs very similar to those used in the
'fute ball' games of the fifteenth and sixteenth century.

space-shuttle *Discovery*, launched from Cape Canaveral, USA. As a pupil, Will demonstrated both academic ability and sporting flair; not only did he excel at rugby but was no mean player on the cricket pitch either.

When the time came for him to leave school Will, by his own admission, just wanted to spend his days chasing an ovoid ball up and down a pitch with 'H' shaped goalposts at either end. But he also realised that there was the small matter of making a living. After studying economics at Durham University he went on to be 'something in the city', working for Midland Global Markets where he was thrown in at the deep end of the world of futures. Later on, however, when the world of professional rugby beckoned the thought of earning his millions as a stock trader was not enough to hold him back. He waved goodbye to 'the pit' and went on to become one of the most successful rugby players England (and Lancashire!) have produced, winning a total of fifty-five caps. But he is has also made it quite clear that, as far as he is concerned, his most treasured memory is of being in the squad that won the 2003 World Cup.

In the list of most-capped players for England, Will Greenwood is ranked third, just behind Jonny Wilkinson and Jason Leonard.

PRINCIPAL
SOURCES

BOOKS

Ackroyd, Peter, *The History of England Vol II*
    (Macmillan, 2012)
Bagley, J.J., *A History of Lancashire* (Phillimore & Co. Ltd,
    1982)
Brighouse, Harold and Charles Forrest, *Hobson's Choice*
    (The Book Clearance Centre, 2001)
Burscough, Margaret, *Historic Fulwood and Cadley*
    (Carnegie, 1998)
Duxbury, Stephen, *The Brief History of Lancashire* (The History
    Press, 2011)
Garlington, John, *Preston* (Chalford Publishing Co., 1995)
Greenhalgh, Malcolm, *Flavours of Lancashire* (Palatine
    Books, 2006)
Greenhalgh, Malcolm, *It Happened in Lancashire* (Merlin Unwin
    Ltd, 2012)
Hole, Christina, *A Dictionary of British Folk Customs*
    (Paladin, 1979)
Hudson, John, *Lancashire of One Hundred Years Ago* (Sutton,
    1993)
Jenkins, Simon, *A Short History of England* (Profile Books, 2012)
Knight, Carole and Stephen Harding, *Viking Mersey*
    (Countryvise, 2002)

Makepiece, Chris, *Lancashire: Events, People and Places Over the 20th Century* (The History Press, 2011)

Mills, A.D., *English Place Names* (OUP, 1993)

Nadin, Jack, *A Grim Almanac of Lancashire* (The History Press, 2011)

Orwell, George, *The Road to Wigan Pier* (Penguin, 2001)

Roud, Steve, *A Pocket Guide to Superstitions of the British Isles* (Penguin Books, 2004)

Whynne-Hammond, C., *English Place-Names Explained* (Countryside books, 2005)

Woodruff, William, *The Road to Nab End* (Eland, 2000)

WEBSITES

www.bbc.co.uk

www.bbc.co.uk/history

www.bbc.co.uk/news/England/Lancashire

www.forl.co.uk

www.imdb.com

www.information-britain.co.uk

www.lancashire.gov.uk

www.manchester2002-uk.com

www.manchester2002-uk.com/ten-towns.html

www.open.ac.uk

www.plant-labels.com

www.spartacus.schoolnet.co.uk

www.wikipedia.org

ACKNOWLEDGEMENTS

First of all I have to thank Michelle Tilling, formerly of The History Press, who offered me this project. Unfortunately she left the company before the book was finished and so was not able to see my efforts through to their conclusion. However, she did continue to offer sound advice (as ever) when she was no longer under any obligation to do so and so I am deeply grateful for her unstinting generosity.

I also have to thank Cate Ludlow, who stepped so agilely into Michelle's shoes as Commissioning Editor, for the way in which she was able to see the task through to what we all hope is a successful completion.

My wife, Jean, and daughter, Kirstine Borrello, also deserve my sincere thanks as they undertook what would have been an impossible task for me – the drawing of many of the little sketches which form such an integral part of the whole piece.

Thank you to the Library of Congress for the use of their extensive picture gallery, and particularly for the use of their images of: King Arthur LC-USZ62–133691, Stephenson's Rocket LC-USZ62–110386 and George Washington LC-USZ62–105109.

If you enjoyed this book, you may also be interested in …

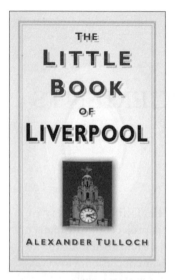

The Little Book of Liverpool

ALEXANDER TULLOCH

Did you know that the clock on the Liver Buildings was started at the precise moment that King George V was crowned on 22 June 1911? Find this and more in Alexander's remarkably engaging book perfect for dipping in to time and time again.

978 0 7524 6006 2

Aintree Days

ALEXANDER TULLOCH

Alexander Tulloch effortlessly evokes life in Liverpool from 1945 to 1962, when he was growing up in a small terraced house in Aintree. Without overdosing on sentimentality he conjures up a world in which all adults seemed to smoke for England, a pint of beer cost a few pence, the 'lav' was a trek across the yard, and where you always went on holiday to Llandudno – an exciting 60 miles away.

978 0 7509 4318 5